The Bigger the Hair, the Closer to God

I absolutely loved this book. Sue Buchanan is one of the finest motivational speakers I know. Combine this with her off-the-chart sense of humor and you have one of the funniest and most poignant books I have read in quite some time.

Jeff Allen
Comedian and author, *My Life as a Bystander*

If you enjoy the witty, tell-it-like-it-is humor of Hallmark's Maxine and the honest faith journey of Anne Lamont's *Traveling Mercies*, you're going to love Sue Buchanan. A survivor of many of life challenges, including breast cancer, Sue pulls no punches here in telling her own story of pain, of searching, and of being afraid, disappointed, amazed, disillusioned, changed, hurt, healed, let down and lifted up again and again. She tells it all with such humor, frankness and transparency that you might find yourself thinking, *Did she just say that?* But you'll also find yourself being encouraged by the insights she shares—insights learned the hard way in the dark and lonely places of life. Sue's chapter on "But, God . . ." (chapter 3) alone is worth the price of the book!

Martha Bolton
Author, *Didn't My Skin Used to Fit?* and *Cooking with Hot Flashes*

How Sue fit that much party between two covers makes me guffaw in wonder! Treat yourself to a spa-sational time while flipping open the lid on your own potential.

Patsy Clairmont
Author, *Dancing Bones . . . Living Lively in the Valley*

Sue Buchanan is hilarious! That girl knows how to turn sacred cows into filet mignon, and she can throw a party you'll never forget! If you want some good laughs on your way to the Pearly Gates, *The Bigger the Hair, the Closer to God* is funnier than sucking helium out of a balloon just before being called on to give the closing prayer at the missionary conference.

Mark Lowry
Comedian, best-selling video *Mark Lowry on Broadway*
Singer and songwriter, "Mary, Did You Know?'

If big hair is a sign of spiritual maturity, Sue Buchanan may be somewhere between Billy Graham and Saint Paul. Oh yes, she has big hair all right—but she also has a big laugh, a big sense of humor, a big heart and something big to say to you about living your life unfettered. She only loves Jesus, her family and friends more than her feather boas and high heels, so strap on your seatbelt and hold on for a wacky ride with a *lot* of profound truth along the way.

Anita Renfroe
Comedian and author, *If It's Not One Thing, It's Your Mother*

I've watched Sue Buchanan at work and in real life, and I've read her books. She is an encourager, a cheerleader, a motivator and one of the craziest women I've ever met. I love that girl!

Lulu Roman
Hee Haw fame, comedian, author and speaker

If you are looking for a quiet, reverent devotional book, I suggest that you quickly put this back on the shelf before anyone sees you with it. If, on the other hand, you are looking to hear from a woman who has walked through some dark places and decided to laugh and live out loud, buy this book immediately. Sue refuses to live in a box, would rather dance than walk, and chooses chocolate over broccoli every day in life. She invites us as readers to join her in living the life out of every day, to be real, to be alive, to be free. It seems to me that is how Jesus lived. So grab your feather boa and read on!

Sheila Walsh
Women of Faith speaker

The Bigger the Hair, the Closer to God

UNLEASHING THE CUTE, WITTY, DELIGHTFUL, INTELLIGENT, PASSIONATE,
AUTHENTIC, INTERESTING, LIFE-OF-THE-PARTY PERSON INSIDE YOU

SUE BUCHANAN

Regal

From Gospel Light
Ventura, California, U.S.A.

Published by Regal Books
From Gospel Light
Ventura, California, U.S.A.
Printed in the U.S.A.

Published in association with the literary agency of WordServe Literary Group, Ltd.,
10152 S. Knoll Circle, Highlands Ranch, CO 80130.

Photography by Deena Graham, Mandy Johnson Studio, Nashville, TN

Library of Congress Cataloging-in-Publication Data
Buchanan, Sue.
The bigger the hair, the closer to God / Sue Buchanan.
p. cm.
ISBN 0-8307-4383-9 (trade paper)
1. Christian women—Religious life—Humor. I. Title.
BV4527.B82 2007
248.8'43—dc22
2006102728

1 2 3 4 5 6 7 8 9 10 / 10 09 08 07

Rights for publishing this book in other languages are contracted by Gospel Light
Worldwide, the international nonprofit ministry of Gospel Light.

Dedication

This book is dedicated to the girls at Hair Villa who glue up my hair and buoy up my spirits. I'm almost always in over my head and working beyond my capabilities, but you, my sweet girlfriends, have given me encouragement when I've been discouraged, complimented me when I didn't deserve it, and made me feel pretty when I felt downright ugly. You've nicknamed me Miss Hollywood and made me believe, at times, I'm really somethin' special.

This book is also dedicated to beauty experts everywhere who work their magic on body and soul. You listen generously and advise well— better than most psychologists and at a fraction of the cost. Here's to you!

And to Carla Retief, my dermatologist (who looks exactly like Angelina Jolie and claims to know a thing or two about reducing the sings of aging), with whom I have a long contract.

Contents

Foreword

By Gloria Gaither

It is risky to write the introduction to this book. In fact, it's risky to have been friends with Sue Buchanan for now going on 40 years. For one thing, you never know when your sweet notes or your "catty" remarks might end up in her next book.

She'll claim to be your best friend, then, just because you're not computer-savvy and refuse to do email, leave you out of the loop when she's confessing to her latest nip 'n' tuck face or body upgrade. You have to read about that in her next book.

I can tell you for a fact that when you read this book and she tells you that if your life's story or spiritual testimony isn't that exciting and you should just exaggerate, she knows where-of she speaks. She has personally embellished some of the dullest stories in history (her history, that is!) and editorialized on events from coast to coast on her self-promoted websites.

And, yes, I'll vouch for it: She doesn't do windows . . . or corners, or window boxes, or . . . And she has a humiliating reputation for sitting in the lap of some perfect stranger just to make his wife or friend or boss think he knows her and then just sachet off down the hall leaving him to come up with an explanation. She might also just show up for some formal hotsy-totsy religious event with one of her famous neon green or hot magenta feather boas flung around her neck and wearing her four-inch red patent leather stiletto heels.

So why am I here to say that you should not only read this book but also buy lots of copies to give to almost everyone you know? Because I love this woman who wears gaudy clothes and pulls ridiculous shenanigans, because she has refused to let some of the toughest blows life can hand out keep her from laughing, eating chocolate and believing in a God who is good, merciful and full of adoration for His children.

Sue and I wept together over her lost girl (who seemed like my child, too) until that child came home. I consoled her when she lost her bust line (and her identity) by reminding her that I never had a bust line and was still in search of an identity. She held me when I thought I couldn't breathe for sadness and told me to "snap out of it" when I wallowed in self-pity. We have both had our share of "Oy vey!" and through it all, we've come to believe that God "doesn't play hide-and-seek with us. He's not remote; he's near. We live and move in him, can't get away from him!" (Acts 17:27-28, *THE MESSAGE*).

Sometimes being "religious" keeps us from this wonderful daily, hourly awareness. Thank God for people like Sue who strip away our trappings and help us bare our very souls to the One who loves us beyond (and sometimes in spite of) our wildest imaginations!

Acknowledgments

To Becky Johnson (you Big-Haired Lady, you!) for suggesting that I write this book and then enthusiastically nudging me in the ribs until it was done.

To Greg Johnson, who is the best agent in the whole world. I'm sorry I fired you that time, but I'm glad I came to my senses and rehired you, because nobody is better at what they do, works harder or is more fun to work with.

To Kim Bangs, who caused me to choose Regal with one sentence: "We really want you, we *love* your writing, and we want you in our catalog!" We've since become girlfriends, as in shopping girlfriends! Yay, us!

Thanks to my daughter Dana Shafer, who edited, offered suggestions and laughed at the appropriate places. Not once did she respond with "Moth-*errrr, pleeease.*"

To Bonnie Shafer and Alice Shillis, who read over my shoulder to make sure I was making sense. I wasn't, but we've decided to go with it anyway.

Bouquets of gratitude go to my friends (Big-Haired Ladies all—you know who you are!), who allow me—*encourage me, for heaven's sakes!*—to be me. Crazy. Offbeat! And yes, even . . . what? . . . iconoclastic, maybe?

Introduction

Not long ago when I first decided to write this book, I fancied myself a sort of self-appointed amateur psychologist. For a few years I'd been traveling around the country, speaking and promoting books, and I'd listened to hundreds of stories from people who had moved beyond crisis and come out the other end with their sanity and their sense of humor intact.

I guess you could say it went to my head.

Why not write down these real-life experiences? I thought. *I'll dissect them, find a formula (a pat answer!) that will work across the board for everyone, and then wrap it up with some deep, profound and insightful conclusions.* (Right there is your first problem. I'm not that deep. I'm shallow! But my friends tell me I'm deep for a shallow person.)

I'd seen books that offered an exercise at the end of each chapter. I could do that! "Do not move ahead to the next chapter until you've accomplished this assignment. Do not pass go; do not collect $200!" The implication being that when you'd read the last page and completed every exercise, you'd wind up being the person you always hoped you'd be. (Instead, I've chosen to do little off-meter limericks. They may not make you the person you hoped to be, but at least you'll have a good laugh and comfort yourself with the fact that you can write better poems.)

In writing my pseudo-psychologist book, I thought I'd shine a spotlight on the folks who've shared their gut-wrenching stories with me. Maybe delve Oprah-style into their pasts. Find out what childhood secrets hold the key to their behavior in times of crisis. Were those who bounced back breast-fed or bottle-fed? Spanked or scolded? The world would thank me, I mused.

Then I realized I'm not a psychologist and never will be. Duh! I barely know a case of schizophrenia from a case of acne, and I only spent two and a half years at college, where I studied music. Even there, I was pretty pathetic. Bottom line: I didn't waste my time studying; I went to college to have a good time. To kiss and be kissed. And while I'm not bragging, yes, I was kissed more times than the Pope's ring. (Wait! I guess I *was* bragging. I sure can't brag about good grades!)

"You're writing about surviving crisis?" asked my agent. "Crisis?" queried my friends. "It's true you've had more than your share, but you're a humorist. Crisis is not a funny subject!" And right they are. Crisis is not a funny subject!

But big hair, I submit, is! *If only I can make that connection,* I thought to myself, *it just might work!* So if you're reading this page in book form, it *did* work. If you're reading from a wadded-up, discarded piece of paper you found in the publisher's trash can, it didn't.

So here I am, on the one hand, not a psychologist—yet someone who has the audacity to play around with the sciences of the mind. And here I am, on the other hand, quite shallow—someone whose very motto says it all: "You can't serve God without a colorful feather boa, a good hairdresser and a Vietnamese nail tech!"

What's a woman like that to do?

Write a big-hair book about her own personal theories, make them entertaining and informative, and then call herself an expert. *Voila!* That's what she does. Writing a book is the quickest way to become a professional know-it-all. So here I come with my expert opinions. And did you happen to know that the etymology (ooooo-eee, love the sound of that word!) of "expert" is this: "x" means unknown and "spurt" is a drip under pressure?

So buckle your seatbelt.

CHAPTER 1

Trading In Your Support Bra for a Feather Boa!

Unleashing the Big-Haired, Livin'-Loud Lady Inside You

Remember the person you planned to be? Thought you *were*, in fact, when you were young and innocent and didn't know any better? Before that thing called "life" grabbed you by the pony-tail, shook you around like a Louisiana hurricane and robbed you of your uninhibited self? Sure you do!

I'm not suggesting you're a wallflower, dear reader, but didn't you plan to be this cute, darlin', witty, chatty, delightful, intelligent, *interesting* (as in life-of-the-party) person for heaven's sake? And puh-leeeze! Far be it from me to push you to be some-thing you're not. But stop and think. Isn't there a *you* in there someplace that's sparkling with personality—a wild filly of a woman who somehow got put out to pasture (or *stabled*, heaven forbid!), made to feel broken and tamed—who's just chomping at the bit to get out? Poised and ready to explode out of the starting gate . . . jumping all the fences? Causing everyone to sit up and take notice?

Don't you wish your *audience* (your friends and acquaintanc-es, of course) would hang on your every word? Maybe even fall on the floor laughing once in a while? (Okay, perhaps you'd settle for just being able to finish a sentence. I know the feeling.)

I call that hidden-away person the Big-Haired Lady Within. And before you jump to conclusions and think otherwise, I'm not claiming to be *all that*—at least not all at once—and if I met somebody who was, I'd probably hate her guts!

We all can claim to be cute, witty, darlin', wise . . . whatever . . . *some* of the time. But doncha think we can also all admit to healthy doses of doubt, fear, questions of self-worth, ugly behavior and—I'll admit it if you will—stupidity? (In fact, you may see all of those things play out right before your eyes in this very book!)

Right here and now, I need to point out that my observations are that of a humorist. Write that down! And remember it when you get your dander up over something I've said.

Better yet, I'm . . . I'm . . . an iconoclast. Write that down, too.

My daughter Dana once called me that, and as you can imagine, I was overwhelmed with pride—honored that my own progeny would speak so highly of me. Then I looked it up in the dictionary and found out it didn't mean I was an "icon of class," as I'd assumed. Instead, I was "a breaker or destroyer of images—one who attacks cherished beliefs and traditional institutions." Oh, my! That's very different! (I also discovered the true meanings of a couple of other words. "Panmixia" means "random breeding" and has nothing in the world to do with "mixing things in a pan," and "misanthrope" doesn't mean "miss the rope" or, extrapolating a bit further—which one tends to do—it doesn't mean "miss the point"! It means "hater of mankind." Who'd a thunk?)

My life's goal is to poke holes in every sacred cow in the pasture. To make us examine everything we believe, sort truth from myth and face the truth. And then, hopefully, everybody—meaning *you* . . . you with the book in your hand and me with the computer screen in my face—can *har-de-har-har* our heads off at some of the silly things we hang on to and that wrongly define us. Or we could just forget the book and head for the outlet mall.

Let's do the book first. Then the mall.

So, I'm an iconoclast. And a humorist! (Just making sure that was clear.) Don't say you weren't warned.

Even the most sedate, soft-spoken and studious among us daydream "what ifs." What if we were a smidge more social? What if we began to speak up and be counted? What if we could bust out of the stereotype? Even just an itsy, bitsy, teen-sy, weensy bit?

Too many of us have long neglected the part of our persona that simply craves more. More what? Depending on your personality, it could be a number of things. Perhaps you crave a college degree (me too! I never quite got around to finishing—and regardless what you may have heard, I wasn't kicked out!), a chance to take voice lessons (*not* me! I tried it once and people laughed), an opportunity to start a business, or maybe just go to a spa and have a makeover. Maybe your inner *out there* woman craves more colorful outfits, bolder earrings, high*er* heeled shoes and fishnet stockings (well, maybe not fishnets). Or a newer (higher?) hairstyle that makes a statement! One of those "the bigger the hair, the closer to God" up-dos that say, "Here I am, y'all! Let the party begin!"

Before I dispense with the subject of hair, I've been told there's a tribe somewhere in the far reaches of the world (Africa maybe—I'm not known for checking my facts) that wears straight-up-in-the-air ponytails and believes these creations to be "of God." (This little factoid has nothing to do with my point, but images fly through my head and I hate not sharing them. My writing style may feel a bit like whiplash if you're a person who prefers to read in chronological, get-to-the-point order, but I say taking the scenic route is what life's all about.

I like to be entertained on the way to The Point! Or duh—what *is* the point? I tend to put on the brakes when I see a sign that says *Giant Alligator Farm and Snake Charmer* on my way to a family reunion. So what I'm saying is, Welcome to the alligator farm of my mind.)

Another aside to the aforementioned aside: Far be it from me to question another person's "of God." You hear that expression all the time here in Nashville, where big hair and big religion are as common as garlic cheese grits at a sit-down dinner. "The song I just wrote is 'of God,' and furthermore, I'm sure it's 'of God' that Martina record it on her next CD!" Here in the rhinestone Bible belt, even parking spots can be "of God." And a parking place right next to TJ Maxx is "*truly of God*"!

Back to the jungle! These tribal members believe their handy coiffeurs make it possible for God, when He is ready, to quickly and easily reach down, grab them by the ponytail and transport them straight to heaven. *Zappo!* No muss! No fuss! No pallbearers!

Fascinating.

Hmmm. Now where were we right before we took a detour through Africa and were dragged through the parking lot at TJ Maxx?

Oh yes! Unleashing that big-haired, livin'-loud lady within you. What does she look like in your mind's eye? What happened to her? Whadaya say we spend some time together in the pages of this book and see if we can't find her and bring her out to play?

You may argue (I can hear you! I have ears on the back of the page), "Sue, you just don't understand. If I unleash the wild side of my personality—the one I've kept so neatly under wraps for these many years—what will my family say? What will my friends think? What will the mugga-muggas at the tennis club think? Or the teachers at my kids' school? Not to mention the goody-two-shoes at church—good-golly-miss-molly!—where I'm a pillar of perfection and from whence I'd be looked down upon for even saying the word 'golly.' They may sing 'This Little Light of Mine.' They may even do the hand motions. They may stamp their feet on the 'no!' part, but don't think for a minute that they really *mean* I should let my little light shine. At least when it comes to my shining personality!"

I say, "Honey, let the tortilla chips fall where they may, and let the salsa splash where it will!" Yes, they'll be suspicious. Sure, they'll try to medicate you. Trust me, they'll get over it. And once the authentic, gorgeous, brilliant you is finally free to fly, you'll thank me.

The cost is worth it—and you betcha there's a cost. Like most everything these days, this book comes with a warning. And I wouldn't be a real friend if I didn't prepare you for opposition. It will come. The price of freedom has never been cheap: not for our country (thank you, soldiers!), not for our souls (thank you, God!) and not for your right to be the full person the Father in heaven created you to be. (Thank *me* because I got you thinking about all this. And by the way, don't send flowers, fruit baskets or bubble bath. Send chocolate!)

Who will oppose the changes you make?

Sadly, it will usually be the people closest to you who will negate who you are and what you're about—the very ones who are supposed to love you most. I'm talkin' parents, husbands, wives, children, teachers, business associates, fellow church members, publishers . . . (that last one will be edited out, I'm sure!).

Sometimes it's the very culture of a family, school or institution that negates us and puts us down. For instance, some of our religious institutions are so steeped in a tradition of conformity that it may as well be written into the by-laws:

1. Make sure our members are never told the truth about God being love. It will cause them to relax. We don't want that.

2. When a member gets out of line, give her a disapproving look or a roll of the eyes, and make saint-like "tsk-tsking" sounds. Words aren't necessary.

3. Enforce the dress code, which is, in brief: Do not be yourself. Look like everyone else.

4. Scare the bejeebers out of them as often as possible. Let them know God's gonna get 'em! Keeps 'em on their toes spiritually.

Repeat after me: "Hooey!"

If your church sounds like that, the good news is you can change churches! This may be painful perhaps, but well worth the effort.

Of course, while you can change churches, you can't change families. (Well, you *can*, but it involves a lawyer, and children can get messed up in the process.) I'm pretty convinced, after talking to thousands of women, that family members often not only negate each other, thwarting each other's true personalities, but they can also be amazingly brutal in the process. There's nothing like a nay-saying family member to make you second-guess yourself, causing gut-sucking insecurities.

Sometimes not-so-subtle disapproval comes from the lower limbs of the family tree—our own kids! Surprise! Surprise! (Like I'm telling you something you didn't know!)

I once showed up at my daughter Dana's high school in a camel-colored suede pantsuit with fox collar and cuffs, intending to dash in and drop off a permission slip. Seems the cute, popular boys who happened to be hanging out in the entryway took notice and for the rest of the day made a huge deal out of the foxy chick mom with the fur around her neck. I never heard the end of it from my firstborn.

"Moth-*errrrr!* I could just die! How could you? Do you always have to be dressed up? You are just too fancy for your own good!"

In an effort to balance the scales, on my next trip to Hillwood High School, I wore wash-the-windows blue jeans (this was years before the everybody's-wearing-them designer-yet-ragged jeans of today). Dana was equally embarrassed.

"Moth-*errr!* You looked like the cleaning lady!" (I *was* the cleaning lady for Pete's sake, whoever Pete is!) Keep in mind that this is the very same, now-grownup daughter who not long ago gave my husband, Wayne, and me a book entitled *Weird Parents*, with this personal inscription: "Mama & Daddy . . . This book pretty much sums up the way I feel about you! Thanks for being very weird parents! Dana." (The book, by the way, is by Audrey Wood. And I suggest that you go straight to Amazon.com, order it and read it out loud to your family. Your children just may get the point and cut you some slack!)

On a more serious note, when you risk being the *real* you— whether it's following your dream or teasing your hair an inch higher than before—you may get some serious harassment (let's call it what it is). However thinly veiled, you know when a comment is just plain ol' malicious and mean spirited. When this occurs, no matter the motivation, no matter how many times you've ignored it in the past, you need to acknowledge that rude is rude and stand up for yourself. Who else is going to? I've found this to be a good response: "The next time you feel compelled to tear me down, please take your fist and hit me in the stomach. It feels pretty much the same." A bold comment, but it's true! Rude comments do feel that way when you're on the receiving end, and shooting straight with a meanie just may turn things around.

The crisis that changed my thinking about who I was and who I wanted to be was breast cancer. Twenty-three years ago, the doctor predicted that I would die before the year was out. So I figured, what did I have to lose? I'd eat all the chocolate I wanted and I'd be me! Perhaps this letting go of "shouldas" and "oughtas" in exchange for my true desires was the prescription that cured me. (Then again, it was bound to be the chocolate. I eat several Hershey bars a day and have for all these years that I've been cancer free.)

Now my itinerary takes me all over the country, speaking to groups of men and women alike about surviving crisis and using it as a springboard to a more authentic, enjoyable life. (Although my crisis was initially breast cancer, trust me and keep reading. I've had more than my share of soap-opera moments!) I'm known to show up at a speaking gig armed with a plethora of feather boas, which I use to decorate the podium as well as any attendees who happen to be standing nearby. I also sell them at my product table—you'd be surprised at how quickly a hot pink feather boa can perk up an otherwise ordinary outfit! Or nightgown! (Ahem . . . cough, cough!)

I tell my audience that my technologically enhanced bosom (wait for the laugh) just got too weighed down with all those little "awareness ribbons" (cancer awareness, AIDS awareness, bring-home-the-troops awareness, sore-throat-and-fever aware-ness, need-a-trim-and-a-perm-and-a-breath-mint awareness) and that I wanted to make a bolder statement. Thus the boas! I say the feather boa is a sign I'm aware. *Aware!* I'm aware of . . . well, pretty much everything.

It's not unusual for me to toss a feather boa into the audi-ence, and it always surprises me how the most seemingly timid person will lunge into the air for it like a Dallas Cowboy cheerleader. Then she flings that thing around herself with a flourish and becomes a new woman. Playful. Flirty. The center of attention!

If you're ready to begin setting your Big-Haired Lady free, may I suggest you begin with a boa?

What's that you say? You don't have one lying around the house? It can be imaginary. Or did I mention I can mail you one from www.suebue.com? (Not that I make a profit on that particular item. I do it for you!)

Once you're wrapped in your brightly colored flock of feathers, give yourself permission to become the passionate, fully alive person you've always wanted to be—divinely empowered to do that thing that you've always dreamed of! Volunteer to care for the penguins at your local zoo, sign up for skydiving class, write a book, learn to paint, enroll in a class, plant a garden, change jobs, change hairdos, get a face life . . . if the shoe fits . . .

If the shoe doesn't fit, *buy new shoes!*

I can't tell you how many letters and emails I've received from women who tell me about the life changes that have resulted from the addition of a feather-boa attitude to their personality wardrobe. Hell*ooo*!

* * *

Unleashing Your Inner BHL!

If a feather boa doesn't tickle your fancy, find, make or buy a symbol that defines or unleashes a part of the real you that's been suppressed, ignored or stuck in a rut.

Leopard-skin underwear? You decide!

Surely some part of you longs to be more creative—that "thing in your gut" part of you that you've allowed to remain dormant. Sometimes the action of just doing something very simple and creative starts the ball rolling. Take a dance lesson, grow an herb garden, start a journal, or buy a set of paints and an easel. One small risk, resulting in a small success.

Before you know it, the doors to your heart will fling open to unleash the real you. Start small. Think big!

A Lame, Lousy Limerick

To hide who you are is a sin.
Don't you wanna be more than you've been?
Visit alligator farms?
Maybe tattoo your arms?
Be that livin'-loud lady within?

A Pithy, Provocative Quote

I gave you life so you could live it!

THE MOTHER, SPEAKING TO HER DAUGHTER TOULA,
IN *MY BIG FAT GREEK WEDDING*

CHAPTER 2

A Kumquat Makes for a Good Friend, and a Lava Lamp Just Might Be the Perfect Gift

Unleashed to Be a Friend

Now that your feather boa is in place, you need an audience. After all, how can you be the life of the party if there's nobody to party with? It's time to evaluate the friendship issue. Who are your friends—and do they know how to party?

You'll have to admit there are loads of books on the subject. Friendship this, friendship that . . . the how-tos, the how-*not*-tos . . . the *ABC*s of friendship. But in the world at large, have these resources helped even one iota? I don't think so!

Most of them are itty-bitty, teeny-tiny gift books filled with meaningless platitudes—those not-worth-the-paper-they're-written-on undersized books that seem to be displayed next to the cash register in every store you go into these days. There's barely any room to make a transaction anymore! Where, pray tell, are you supposed to put your wallet while you swipe your card? In your armpit, maybe?

Either these poor-excuse-for-a-book books are multiplying during the nighttime hours when the stores are closed, or folks are snapping them up in record numbers. I've heard that stores put product near the cash register to target those "impulse buyers" who just can't help themselves. My impulse would be to take those books and—well, never mind.

They're even sold at the checkout counter of my carwash down on White Bridge Road, and last Christmas they added impulse handbags to the mix! Handbags at a carwash? Can you *believe* it? And not just any handbags—I'm talkin' Prada! Yves! Even Doonsberry! These weren't knock-offs, either—they were the real thing. I have a good eye for such things and, yes, the prices were really low, and, yes, there were a few loose threads hanging off the seams, but trust me, they were real! I know my merchandise.

It was very last minute—like maybe two days before Christmas—and I still had names on my list not checked off and no bright ideas. So, as you can imagine, I was ecstatic. It was almost like an answered prayer—and would have been had I prayed, but I'd not yet gotten to that point. I was close, though.

Becky, check! Cara, check! Kirby, check! Wow! Maybe one for Mindy. And my impulse said that Dana would like a small one. And at the carwash! Unreal! I didn't even have to pray for a parking spot.

Christmas came and went, and the purses were the hit of the day. January rolled around, and one cold winter night, I noticed my husband foaming at the mouth, muttering words that I couldn't make out and waving something that looked very much like a credit card bill. I listened closely.

"Those MasterCard people! Those half-wits! You gotta check every single transaction line by line. Then when you catch 'em red-handed they won't even admit their mistake! How could *anybody* charge $179.89 at a *car wash*? You'd think it would be obvious. How could anyone miss *that*?"

By this time, Wayne was red in the face and, as if to prove his point and gain an ally, was jabbing his finger at the bill right under my nose. "Look at this! Those morons! I called and gave

them what for, and they said they'd look into it. *Look into it?*
LOOK INTO IT!? What's there to look into?"

"Umm, 'scuse me?" I asked sweetly, "What were you saying?
You say you *called* them?" (*Eeek!* I thought. *How do I get out of this
one.* With honesty, straightforwardness and a little batting of
the eyelashes, that's how!)

"Darlin'. Honey. I think it really *might* be possible to spend
$179.89 at a car wash. Let me explain . . . There were all these
darlin' little friendship books that distracted me. And then,
once distracted, I noticed these *fabulous* designer purses. And
they weren't just any purses! I'm talkin' Prada and—"

Well, dear reader, you don't wanna know the rest of it. (And
it didn't even end with good ol' let's-just-make-up sex!) But back
to the friendship books and another thing that gets my goat.
Just show me one that's devoid of flowers on the cover and I'll
shut up. And correct me if I'm wrong, but within the pages, by
way of prose or poetry, there's always the inevitable comparison
of a friend to a—go ahead, gag me with a spoon—a flower.

Think about it for a minute. When was the last time you
picked up a book that compared a friend to a fruit? Maybe
something like this:

You are a bright and shining kumquat in my life. Even
though you've been in the vegetable bin a bit too long,
I think of you not as slimy but as shining. And there's a
world of difference . . . friend! The tender touch of
mold reminds me that you aren't quite perfect, and
that's a comforting thought, because I'm not perfect
either . . . friend! We are fellow strugglers together . . .
my kumquat friend!"

Doesn't rhyme, but so what? Time is at a premium—I have
a book deadline. Besides, I'm pretty sure that particular style

of poetry is universally accepted and even has an official name. Free fall? Free bird? Free for all? I'll check with Joy—she's my grammarian friend. Which causes me to stop here and make my first point about friendship: *Choose friends who know more than you do.* That way, you don't have to remember everything yourself.

Just pick up the phone. "Hey, Alice, should I be usin' oil or Crisco in my fryin' pan these days? Get back to me ASAP! The kids are home and asking for fried chicken and dumplings, and it's been years!"

Before I get too carried away criticizing friendship books, I should probably 'fess up: I've written several. Keep in mind, however, that mine are different. One is called *Girls Gotta Have Fun! 101 Great Ideas for Celebrating Life with Your Friends*, and, unlike many others in the genre, it has no profusion of cabbage roses on the jacket—it has a cat.

In addition, my book is printed in a larger format than the others, so you won't always be losing it down in the cushions of the sofa. Perhaps that's the reason I'm on such a rampage in the first place. *Duh!* Those runty little mini-sized books disappear! When I cleaned house four (or seven?) years ago, I found 62 of them in the couch alone. One had sprouted, reaching its poor little dried-up pages upward and outward toward the window light.

There are two other friendship books that I've coauthored (*Friends Through Thick and Thin* and *Confessions of Friends Through Thick and Thin*) with my friends Joy, Gloria and Peggy. One of those, I must admit, has flowers on the cover and uses gardening as a metaphor throughout. Yack! Not my idea!

What can I say? I was strong-armed. Railroaded!

Actually, and I say this with a humble spirit, I was the one who was the most flexible and peace loving—the first to display true Christian virtues in the decision-making process.

Yes. That was it. Thus (lo and behold!) emerges my second point, dear reader, and it comes in two parts: *When it comes to dealing with friends, (1) choose your battles, and (2) sometimes just graciously give in.* (Especially when it's three against one.)

Although our book talks about gardening, Peggy is the only true gardener of the bunch. She has ugly hands to prove it! She says her Johnny Jump-Ups grin at her. Mine grimace!

No gardening for Gloria. She has a yard boy! Remember the gardener from *Desperate Housewives*? Yup, he looks like that kind of yard boy. Gloria sits on her porch, rockin' away in her big white wicker rocker, reading Dostoyevsky with one eye and watchin' the yard boy with the other.

Joy is the least likely gardener in our foursome. One day when we were sitting around her pool admiring her big pots of healthy geraniums, Peggy said, "Look at Joy's geraniums. It's been an unusually hot summer. I can't believe how full and healthy Joy's plants are."

When we got up out of our chairs and took a closer look, we found that they were fake! And surprisingly, Joy had no problem admitting it. "I get them at the funeral home outlet," she informed us in her schoolteacher voice, as though she was expecting us to take notes or something. "They truly do look fuller and healthier than real flowers."

Which brings me to point number three: *Don't disdain your friends' choices, be it funeral outlet flowers, lava lamps or a Plaster of Paris wall-hanging of the Last Supper.* Or big hair! As Barbara Streisand once said, "You salt my peas and I'll salt mine, too." Or something like that. In other words, everybody doesn't like the exact same things, and something so insignificant shouldn't stand in the way of friendship.

The fourth point is to *forget everything you know about gossip being all bad.* Gossip has gotten a bad rap! And before you raise your eyebrows (they need a good plucking by the way) and start making those tsk-tsking noises with your tongue, hear me out.

Gossip is what makes the world go round, and it's not that bad if you really know what you are doing. Even when reading *People* (the Queen Mother of gossip mags), don't you occasionally find something downright edifying? Heartwarming even? Like when the couple from Peoria took in 72 foster kids who were all in iron lungs, had their teeth straightened and their eyes corrected, got them good haircuts and gave them a bed and three square meals a day?

The important thing to know is that I'm not talkin' about mean, wicked, malicious gossip—or makin'-somethin'-up-just-for-the-sake-of-makin'-it-up gossip. *I'd never!* I'm talking *newsy* gossip.

For instance, I might call Janet and Carlene and say, "Susie is on another one of her bike trips. France this time! Taking a barge up the Rhine with stops along the way to cycle the back roads and soak in the beauty of the countryside."

The key is to say it with great admiration. It's only when you say "*crazy* bike trips" and finish your sentence with "can you believe *thaaaaat?*" that it becomes wrong. (You can still roll your eyes, however—they can't see it over the phone line.)

Saying things like "Can't she just bike to the Piggly-Wiggly and back like the rest of us, for Pete's sake?" *Wrong!* Or, "Well, Jim died and left her all that money. She's probably on the make for a new husband—a Frenchman who can't even speak English maybe. That would be like her." *Wrong!*

That's gossip! Unadulterated gossip!

Ready for point number five? (Are you with me here, or still hung up on the gossip issue? Girl, get over it!)

Point number five is: *Support your friend in her pursuit of happiness, whatever that happiness might be.* I'm not talking about being her accomplice in an axe murder, of course—or approving her taking a job in a strip club. You know what I'm saying. Support the crazy bike trip. Be a bridesmaid when she marries the Frenchman. Even support the plastic surgery, if that's what she wants.

When you live in Nashville, it's not unusual to run into a friend at the symphony, at church or at the grocery store and realize that something is different. The problem is that you aren't quite sure *what's* different. Your friend looks rested. Her face looks a bit younger. The truth is, her face is so tight you wonder if her eyebrows will move when she adjusts her socks. Or perhaps there's been a drastic narrowing of the waistline. Or a waistline where one hadn't existed before (at least not since junior high school).

What happened to those saddlebags ample enough to carry supplies into the Grand Canyon for a week-long donkey ride without the donkey? Could it be support hose? A galvanized-rubber body stocking?

What about that once-nondescript straight-up-and-down figure that's become downright voluptuous? As in cleavage a small child could smother in. As in "Please, let me tie your shoelace for you. I'm sure you can't see your feet anymore." Do you mention it or do you avert your eyes? An especially difficult choice when you're standing at the produce counter trying to choose a melon, wondering if it's a Miracle Bra or a miracle of the TBN variety.

Twenty years ago, I had plastic surgery to fix my body after a mastectomy. I got two perky new breasts with a tummy tuck thrown in. I don't understand why women—and men (you'd be surprised!)—don't just admit it when they've had "work" done!

To me, plastic surgery is like going to the dentist. If there's a problem with your tooth—like you broke it off when you were eating a Sugar Daddy—you get it fixed. If there are ruts in your face, think Botox. If something's drooping? Duh!

As for me, my face is drooping, so I've decided that rather than shock my friends with one big surgery, I'll approach it a little at a time—have a few small procedures done here and there and keep them abreast (pun intended) on a regular basis. None of this *did she or didn't she?* for me.

The first step in this process was to get blepharoplasty, which is removing the fat from around the eyes. It was nothing! You sit down in this big comfy chair that's designed to fool you. After you're asleep, it tilts back and becomes an operating table. You get a shot that makes you feel wonderfully woozy, and then you wake up an hour later and go to Sonic and eat two corn dogs for lunch (which is what I dreamed about while I was under anesthesia). Yes, for a couple of days I looked as if I'd lost the WWF tournament. And yes, my eyes were bloodshot and my cheeks were a little bruised for a couple more days. But after that I looked pretty good.

Did I hide what I'd done? No! I announced it in a news release sent out to special friends by email, which said:

> Author/speaker Sue Buchanan announces her recent plastic surgery (eyes only) to better serve Jesus! Prior to the procedure, Buchanan faced the soul-searching dilemma of whether to request prayer and fasting on her behalf, but she was advised by those close to her that one simply doesn't ask for prayer for an eyelift. Buchanan is recovering nicely in her Nashville home. For interviews, please call her publicist, Elmer Fardquark.

The responses were priceless!

From my son-in-law: "Laughed out loud. A Scripture in Ephesians says, 'May the eyes of your heart be enlightened.' You could probably take that to mean: 'May the eyes of your face be heightened.'"

My brother Joe wrote: "After wrestling with the theological implications of invoking the Almighty to intervene in the human pursuit of vanity, we did pray for you. Hope you are recovering nicely and that you'll soon have that face back in the flare of the Kleigs."

One friend who's a real, honest-to-goodness publicist said: "Who is this Elmer? I'm your publicist! Shall I service this to the trades and consumer? Or trades only? Let me know."

From fellow speaker Lee Ezell: "Dear Elmer, please get word to Ms. Buchanan that God *is* into the *faith lift* business and is 100 percent behind her efforts." I guess she mistook the word "face" for "faith."

My most recent procedure was to better define my chin line— if I hear the words "turkey neck" one more time, all I can say is, it better be Thanksgiving!

See the camaraderie of friendship? You! I'm talking to you! Do you know how easy it would have been to keep all of this a secret and miss the fun of it? To keep the friendship game going (and to remain mentally stable), you've gotta keep looking for things to laugh about. And that's my next point, number six: *Choose friends you can laugh with*. Yes, choose friends you can laugh with . . . at anything, everything and nothing at all.

Point number seven is worth the price of the book! It will show you how to be so interesting that everyone will jump over tables (or hedges or pews) to be your friend. And it's as easy as falling off a log: *Always have something interesting to talk about*.

If your conversation well is a little dry, *read book jackets*. Before you make your debut as the most fascinating and knowledgeable (not to mention witty, cute and darlin') person in the room, go to a bookstore and read the jackets of books that are considered cutting-edge. Find one statement that you can use as a conversation starter. For instance, from the flyleaf of *The Lexus and the Olive Tree* by Thomas L. Friedman, you could glean (and use) this insight: "Wow, you know you simply cannot understand the morning news or know where to invest your money unless you understand how globalization is shaping the world and the tensions it creates with the ancient forces of culture. Am I right?"

Obviously you'll have to have different ploys for different audiences. For a simple coffee klatch: *Read* People *magazine*. Absorb bits of information about famous people. Remember, you only need a nugget. Then say, "I was reading just this morning . . ." (Don't say *where* you were reading! Duh!) ". . . that St. Tropez seems to be the vacation spot of choice for the rich and famous this year. Wonder how that compares to where we go? We've always gone to Myrtle Beach. Last year we upgraded from the Motel 6 to the Red Roof."

Keep the discussion going with interesting items like money-saving tips—as in how important it is to strap a cooler full of pop to the top of the SUV because drinks cost double at the beach. Have pointers ready on how to best cover your tummy roll and still go out during daylight hours—as in what a blessing those cute, funky T-shirts are with the skinny-waisted body in a bathing suit stamped on them, front and back.

If the subject of "brilliant children" comes up (and, 'scuse me, doesn't it *always*?), with some slight of hand, you can manipulate the conversation straight to architecture. Follow me, dear reader. When playing with sand, all children are architecturally gifted. So you say, "Speaking of architects, have you been following the career of Zaha Hadid? They said she was merely a 'paper architect,' but she sure showed them, didn't she?"

Here's another way to have things to talk about: Become proficient at *clicking the clicker—never watch a TV show in its entirety*. Do you even know why God gave us the remote control? To click back and forth and gain as much information as possible in the briefest amount of time. Again, duh! For example, watching 60 seconds of the Weather Channel will tell you that there was a tornado in Kansas and that a girl in red shoes is missing, along with her little dog, Toto. This will give you three topics to talk about: weather, pets and shoes.

Naturally, I'd choose shoes.

A couple of minutes with Nancy Grace and you'll know who was murdered and where and who the suspect is. Need I tell you? Murder is a hot, hot topic. And you'll only have to watch Wolf Blitzer ('scuse me . . . *Wolf?* What kind of a name is that?) for a second or two to get a read on the political situation. That is, if your psyche can possibly handle all the wild multimedia dynamics coming at you at once. All those screen configurations! All those men and women of every color and creed and hair-do out on the scene with their fancy-shmantzy remotes! And the graphics? Spinning, zooming, crawling graphics so intense you're likely to end up at the chiropractor with a case of spinning, zooming, crawling whiplash.

Okay, never mind everything you've read so far. Let's just cut to the chase. Here's the shortcut to becoming Queen of Big Hair, able to speak with authority on practically any subject. I'd be remiss it I didn't tell you, so lean in close.

Whenever I'm at any kind of gathering, I table hop (or pew hop, as the case may be). And as I hop, I pick up information. A smidgen of this, a nugget of that. Politics, home and garden, health tips, pertinent news items, to-the-point book reviews, church stuff (I pay special attention to prayer requests). Then, at the next stop, I simply repeat what I've heard as if I know what I'm talking about.

Try it! You too will be thought of as a world authority on pretty much everything. They'll hang on your every word! You may even be *in People* magazine.

But enough about that. On to point *numero eighto*—which, my friend, is the most important of all in your quest for making friends, keeping friends and being a friend. It's simply this: *Be there!*

I've experienced breast cancer and chemotherapy, and I know the havoc it brings. My heart ached as I watched my daughter deal with cancer, which is worse than going through it yourself. I've felt as though I wanted to die because of the helplessness I experienced trying to encourage my other daughter, who for years made wrong decisions. There were divorces in my family that broke my heart. A business gone awry. Family conflicts that seemed more than I could bear. Christmases ruined because of them.

I couldn't have gone through any of these difficulties on my own. My friends were always there for me. At times, they did all the work it took to stay connected. They did all the praying when my own supplications seemed to be getting no higher than the ceiling fan. Those dear, precious ones wrapped their love around me and held on tight. And when the time was right, they helped me pile up my big hair, gave it a shot of hairspray, set me back on my feet and pulled me back into reality.

Leigh Benson-Greer, my friend Peggy's daughter, put it this way:

> When I was a child, I thought friendship was about having fun, talk, laughter-filled sleepovers and long days at the pool. There was no way for me to know how much more friendship would mean to me as I grew older. I began to realize it the day we buried my father. Three hours before the funeral, my friend Brenda came to my door, and almost literally physically supported me through the worst day of my life.[1]

* * *

Unleashing Your Inner BHL!

Click on my website and order *Girls Gotta Have Fun! 101 Great Ideas for Celebrating Life with Your Friends*. You'll find ideas to put

into practice, such as: "When a friend needs you, drop everything and go! Everything does *not* include a chocolate soufflé
or a bottle of hair color . . . and certainly not the baby." Or
"Write a history of your friendship. Begin, 'Once upon a time in
the olden days . . .'" Or how 'bout this one: "When your friend
is busy, offer to take her car to be washed. If the car is a fancy-
schmanzy sports car, take it for a spin before you return it. Poke
her in the ribs, wink and say, 'They were lined up for miles at
the car wash.'" There are 98 more where those came from.

A Lame, Lousy Limerick

At times your friend gives you the irks
But what about all of *your* quirks
If you think quid pro quo
And forgive as you go
"Putting up with" is one of the perks!

A Pithy, Provocative Quote

*I value the friend who for me finds time on his
calendar, but I cherish the friend who for me does
not consult the calendar.*
ROBERT BRAULT

Note
1. Leigh Benson-Greer, *Friends Through Thick and Thin* (Nashville, TN: Zondervan
   Publishing Company, 1998).

I'm Stuck in My Crisis, and I Can't Get Up!

Unleashing Yourself from What Holds You Back . . . Step by Step by Step!

"Whoa," you say. "Hold on there, Nellie. I'm only up to chapter 3 and I already have my nose out of joint! Stupid book. It'll be on the shelf at Melvin's Used and Rare Book Store by nightfall. An idiotic feather boa? *Me?* Not on your life. And furthermore, God knows I'm not looking for an audience! *Me?* Life of the party? Yeah, sure. Go away!" (I can *hear* you.) "Yes, I should put some of that kumquat friendship into practice, but you don't know my life!"

I'm sayin', "Well, maybe I *do* know your life."

Do you grind your teeth and clench your fists when you think of the person you intended to be—and aren't? Are you sorry I brought it up?

When I say that you can unleash the cute, witty, delightful, intelligent, passionate person inside you, do you gag at the word "cute"? Do you take issue with "witty"? (You must be kidding, you say.) "Delightful"? (Don't make me laugh!) "Intelligent"? (Well, maybe a long time ago, when I still used my brain.) "Passionate"? (Don't even *go* there . . . and by the way, what do you *mean* by passionate?)

Hmmm.

Perhaps we should take a step back and acknowledge that sometimes the problem isn't with wit or with passion. We've just gotten stuck in a crisis. We've become paralyzed and can't seem to move our little fingers—let alone put on feather boas or change our hairdos.

I've been there. Maybe you have, too. I've teetered on the edge of that precipice called "I just want to be dead" and felt the wind howling at my back.

But . . .

And it was the "but" that saved my life!

Such a little word to have such potential life-changing impact! *Merriam-Webster's* says that the word "but" means "on the contrary, except for, save, only, unless, if not, yet, except for the fact that, however, nevertheless, still, in spite of." This little word implies that in spite of whatever disaster has come before, *there is still a chance for a different outcome.*

Hey! Did you hear that? Because of one little "but," there is still a chance for a different outcome.

Life had me paralyzed . . . *but* there were those who wedged themselves between me and the cliff with something as simple as a casserole or a card. *But* I had family and friends who loved me and counted on me. *But* someone took time to listen. *But* for a C. S. Lewis book that became my solace. *But* for a girlfriend who taught me to celebrate under very *unc*ele-bratory conditions. *But* for the distraction of my writing and my journaling. *But* for the presence of God, even in the darkest of times.

But for humor! Somewhere in the depths of me there was humor, and it bubbled to the surface and saved my sanity, if not my very life. Granted, my sense of humor *is* a little bizarre. (Oh, no! Surely not!) In fact, it reared its quirky head in the titling of this book. I wanted to call it simply *BUT!* based on the premise I may not be the bold, I-can-handle-what-life-hands-me, Big-Haired Lady at the moment, but there's still a chance for a different outcome.

BUT!

You can see the problems with a title like this—the first of which is finding a publisher. They'd boycott me like I boycotted Wendy's after the finger incident! And if by some chance *BUT!* were published, people would surely mistake it for the word "butt." They'd tell me stories about their husbands, their bosses, or (heaven forbid!) their hemorrhoids! Just think of the jokes I'd have to endure. And can you imagine the media interviews? "We're sorry, Sue. We thought you were a proctologist."

Still, whatever the risk of misinterpretation, keep in mind there's a world of recovery in that three-letter word "but." So much so that you may one day find me teaching "But Certification" classes. (Okay, maybe not!)

"But" is the word I've heard over and over again as I've listened to grieving parents who've lost children to death or mental illness; as I've gotten acquainted with those precious souls who have lost their health, homes and even a husband or wife; as I've commiserated with those who've lost a breast or a testicle (yes, you heard that right). I've comforted those who've experienced perhaps the greatest loss of all—the loss of their hopes and their dreams. "But" was the bridge between despair and living again.

"But . . ." they've explained to me, "I kept telling myself, if I can just get out of bed and put one foot in front of the other!"

"But . . . if I can just do something that doesn't require a brain, like open a can of soup or feed my cat."

"But . . . for my love of music."

"But . . . for my children—or my friends."

"But . . . I just had to laugh in spite of myself."

"But . . . for my faith! For prayer!"

"But . . . for God."

Perhaps a tsunami of a crisis has consumed you and you feel helpless. You feel impotent, barely able to function or even do the normal things in life such as climb out of bed or get yourself bathed and dressed. Putting one foot in front of the other is a monumental effort. If so, know that you aren't alone. There are those who never get over it, whatever the "it" may be, and never again live a life of fullness and hope.

For those who choose to move on (and that's you, isn't it?), the path is not an easy one. And it can't be done in one fell swoop. Getting unleashed from the thing that holds you back is often accomplished in increments—step by step by step—one task building on another.

Sometimes a person can muster what it takes to make an immediate turn-around, but rarely. Since we're thinking in terms of buts and butts, I can't help referring to the story of the Three Billy Goats Gruff. (Simple truths can be found in simple places; I call it Fairytale Therapy.)

Remember how Mr. "I'm going to eat you for breakfast" Troll intimidated each of the goats as they tried to cross the bridge to the place where lush, sweet grass could be found? Remember how the first two barely made it by the skin of their teeth, promising the troll they'd be far more delicious on the return trip after they'd fattened up a bit? Remember how the biggest Billy Goat Gruff, when confronted by the life-threatening, ugly troll, simply lowered his horns, galloped along the bridge and butted? Recall how that obnoxious troll was wiped out forever? Up, up, up in the air he went, and down, down, down into the rushing river. Never to be heard from again!

Yay, big Billy Goat Gruff!

Perhaps the best "but" of all really is a "butt"—as in lowering your head and doggedly (goatedly?) determining to get through the valley, over the bridge and to the other side.

Here's my point: Whether you hit your obstacles head on

like a billy goat or take your time grabbing one "but" at a time, hang on, my friend. Hang on for dear life! There really is a chance for a different outcome.

* * *

Unleashing Your Inner BHL!

It's thinking time. That's all that's required: just thinking. Think about something—*anything!*—that could serve as a "but" in your life, be it a book, a friend, a funny CD or an exercise class. Spend a few minutes each day planning how to leverage that "but" in order to break loose from the rut you're in.

Now take out a piece of paper and draw a bridge. Write down all the things that are keeping you on one side of the bridge (things like "but I'm frightened"). On the other side of the bridge, write out the positive "buts" (things like "but my friends care" or "but God cares!"). Think of yourself as Big Billy Goat Gruff, capable of butting your way out of your fears, addictions and losses and into the promise of lush, green pastures of peace and joy.

A Lame, Lousy Limerick

When life is askew and it's tough
And you've been stuck in the mire long enough
It may take some guts
To start looking for *buts*
(And I don't mean as in Billy Goats Gruff!)

A Pithy, Provocative Quote

A ship in the harbor is safe, but that is not
what ships are built for.
WILLIAM SHEDO

CHAPTER 4

The Little Engine that Could (Until She Couldn't)

Unleashing Yourself Through Crazy Self-Talk

I've always thought that talking to yourself was perfectly normal. It only becomes a problem when you start *answering* yourself! In fact, talking to yourself is one of the best ways I know of to help bring out the BHL within.

"Just a goshdern minute!" you say. "I'm supposed to unleash the Big-Haired Lady in me by *talking* to myself?"

Before you think me wazy (that word is not original with me; another author thunk it up, and it means "way crazy"), let's consider the possibilities.

My life was nearly perfect before I was diagnosed with breast cancer. I had the white picket fence, the dogwood tree and all that went with it. I'd experienced the joy of being a full-time wife to my husband, Wayne, and what seemed at the time to be more-than-a-full-time job as mother to my two daughters, Dana and Mindy.

I could entertain with one hand tied behind my back. Whip up a cake or a pie at the drop of a spatula! And design the most creative Halloween costume on the block from nothing more than an old tablecloth and a pound of Maybelline!

Beyond these talents, I was also a BFF (best friend forever) in a crisis. I saw myself as a regular hip-hip-hooray-wave-the-pom-poms cheerleader for anyone in need of encouragement.

Truth be told, I was probably no encourager at all. In fact, I may even have been a *discourager* with my insensitive, "Oh, it can't be *that* bad!" brand of support. Eager to pronounce my glib platitudes to anyone who would listen, my subliminal message was, "Be like me! Look on the bright side—and have a perfect life! And oh, by the way, here's a macaroni casserole. Return the dish when it's convenient. Enjoy!"

"Don't mullygrub," I always said to my kids when they were having a down day. "Snap out of it!" I'd command when someone had a setback and was feeling depressed.

How those words have come back to haunt me! At best, they've become family lore. Not long ago I said, "Snap out of it!" (*jokingly!*) to my grown daughter Dana. To which she wearily replied, "Mother, *puh-leeze!* I've snapped out of it so often I feel like a big rubber band."

I loved being a stay-at-home mom, but when my children were in junior high and high school, I had time on my hands. So I went out and found myself an adventuresome career. It was the opportunity of a lifetime! I was vice president of a company that specialized in film and video production, corporate meeting planning, and computer authoring and Internet services.

Our clients were often of the Fortune 500 variety, and it wasn't unusual for me to fly off on a corporate jet to work my magic on a client's image and market position. I once showed up to pitch a concept to a bunch of Wall Street blue-suits and passed around a bunch of fans. You know those cardboard face fans? Have you seen the one of Minnie Pearl, complete with the big hat and that dangling price tag? Well, it was pretty funny to look around the table and see 20 Minnie Pearl faces smiling back at me. I got the job!

My life wasn't a total bed of roses, though. I had all the normal ups and downs. My husband and I went through some rough patches. I lost family members who were dear to me, both to death and divorce. My father's passing away was particularly devastating; he died of cancer (a kind that is now 95 percent curable) at the young age of 52. Occasionally, business accounts I'd worked hard to sell slipped through my fingers, and for a time I'd feel as though it were the end of the world. But the earth kept spinning, and somehow I could always summon my best Pollyanna spirit and *snap out of it!*

On the inside, I buried a lot of hurts. But on the outside, I coped, behaving as though the biggest crisis in my life was trying to get my Tupperware back from the person to whom I'd taken baked beans. It was the diagnosis of breast cancer that would ultimately take the wind out of my cheer-up-and-get-on-with-it sails, tip over the boat, and give me a dunk in the drink to boot. For me, it wasn't just that I had cancer; it was the fact that I was losing a body part (a rather *large* body part, mind you) that was devastating to me.

My breast.

It would be no exaggeration to say that from junior high school on, I'd had a misplaced identity. It was the Marilyn Monroe era after all, and because my body and the bodies of my friends were metamorphosing right before our eyes, it was all we thought about.

Neil Simon's Broadway play *Brighton Beach Memoirs* captured it best. Eugene M. Jerome, the 15-year-old lead character, is alone in his upstairs bedroom, where he's fantasizing equally about his role as star pitcher for the New York Yankees and seeing a girl's bare breasts.

"What I'm about to tell you next," he says, "is so secret and private that I've left instructions for my memoirs not to be opened until thirty years after my death. If I had a choice between a tryout with the Yankees and actually seeing her [Margaret's] bare breasts for two and a half seconds, I would have some serious thinking to do."

And since Eugene's favorite food is ice cream, he thinks seeing a girl's breasts and eating ice cream at the same time would be the ultimate experience. (Note to publisher: Get your research department to follow up on this. Do middle-aged men—my readers' *husbands,* for heaven's sake—*really* obsess about *ice cream?* Since it's the new millennium, might it be *sushi*?)

Anyway.

Eugene's obsessions were not unlike those of the kids at my junior high school. For the girls it was, "When will I have them?" "How big will they be?" "Will it happen overnight?" And on and on and on.

For me, the question of it happening overnight was decisively answered one morning when I woke up and found that I had *not* rolled over on the cat but, miraculously, had discovered two mounds of me that hadn't been there the day before. One day I was flat as a pancake. The next, my mother was hustling me off to the department store, where I was fitted for my first bra.

In those days you were "fitted" by matronly ladies who spoke in whispers, ducking in and out of the dressing room with various styles and sizes. None of this buying underwear off the rack in a public place like we do today. Heaven forbid! Someone might see you! The styles were few, colors were not an option, and the word "sexy" was never considered, much less voiced. "Garments," they were called. "Sturdy, durable, maximum coverage *garments.*" Those were the operative words.

My first bra was a 32*B*! Some kids skip a grade in school. I on the other hand . . . (oh, never mind!). The same day we purchased bras, my mother bought me a fashionable hunter-green sweater and coordinating plaid skirt. We giggled as I stood sideways in front of the mirror and admired my changing anatomy. The next day, in my spiffy new outfit, I made a speech to my seventh-grade class, declaring all the ways I'd change the world if they'd elect me their class president.

Afterward, as I made my way to the back of the auditorium, I saw one of the boys take a quick look around to see if anyone was watching. Then he lunged toward my brand-new body with both hands for the quickest squeeze in history!

It made me feel sleazy. And confused.

By the time I went to college, I was a 32C. And I'll never forget discovering, along with my girlfriends, that our boyfriends had created the mythical "perfect woman" from our body parts. The goddess they envisioned was made up of one girl's beautiful face, another's shapely legs and yet another's thick, shiny hair.

Guess what part of *me* made up the perfect woman?

Ah, maybe it's not so bad after all! I thought, and right then and there, big boobs became my identity. Heavens! It was the first thing anyone noticed, so why not joke about it? (I once had a picture taken with Dolly Parton, and . . . *ahem!* Let's just say I gave Dolly a run for her money.)

So you can see why losing a breast was monumental to me. I felt mutilated. Disfigured. Undesirable. For a brief moment in time, I felt as though I might not want to live. Learning about reconstructive surgery changed my mind!

The reality of the cancer diagnosis finally did sink in when I discovered my doctor's notes and found myself face to face with the possibility that I might be dying. There were times during those 12 months of chemotherapy and its side effects when I truly wanted to give up.

That was when I put self-talk to the test and discovered how powerful it can be. The little pep talks I gave myself are what kept me going—putting one four-inch heel in front of the other. "Snap out of it," I'd say. "You can make it! I don't know how, but somehow you'll get through this!"

I learned self-talk as a child. Prodded by a father who was our hometown's perpetual salesman of the year (the man lived and breathed positive thinking!), motivational books had been my bedtime reading for as long as I could remember. "Chug! Chug! Puff! Puff!" went the little red train in what was possibly the world's very first self-help book, *The Little Engine That Could*. Complete with eyes, ears and a pert little nose, the winsome train sure *looked* as if he could. But try as he might, he . . . just . . . *couldn't!* He was broken down, stopped dead in his tracks, and he couldn't budge another inch.

Even as a small child, I knew a crisis when I saw one. It was depressing, and Prozac wasn't an option! It hadn't even been invented. Here was this happy little engine—happy because of the joyous load it was carrying: Christmas toys and treats for the little boys and girls on the other side of the mountain—and it was stuck.

The pictures were vivid: Boxcars full of goodies. Dolls and clowns and sailboats! Balls, books, music boxes, tops and musical instruments. Giraffes with necks stretching to the clouds and fat elephants squished tightly against fuzzy brown bears! A circus monkey scratching its head and looking confused. Every picture is etched in my mind.

Not only could the little engine not move, but he also could not find anyone to lend him a hand. Each time another bigger engine came by and he begged for help, he was rejected. Rejected, negated and made fun of.

The engine is desolate. The dolls are crying. The animals are about to give up. And I (the small child) am waiting for the page to turn. My mama and daddy have read this book to me a hundred times, and even though my little heart is pounding out of my body, I'm pretty sure I know what's going to happen next ("pretty sure" because I didn't yet know for certain that once a book is in print, the story never changes). I can't wait!

I cross my fingers once again, hoping that a compassionate little blue engine will come along—a not very strong or important engine—and that his heart will be touched by the sad plight of the train. Even though he's never been over the mountain in his whole life, he'll give it a try! He'll hitch himself to that little engine and with sheer willpower—and several pages of "I think I cans"—do the impossible! He'll take the train over the mountain and save Christmas for all humanity!

"I think I can, I think I can," I said as I worked to accomplish childhood tasks. Finishing my vegetables. Picking up my toys.

"I thought I could, I thought I could," I said as I walked from the doctor's office, having had a dozen stitches sewed into my forehead without the benefit of painkillers.

"I thought I could, I thought I could," I said bravely when I finally learned to ride a two-wheeler. As for my potty training? Do I have to tell you? It was the tried and true think-I-can-thought-I-could method that worked for me, my brothers and even my own children. I highly recommend it.

When my father died, I allowed myself to be sad, to grieve. But inevitably I pushed forward, saying to myself, "You've mullygrubbed long enough. Pick yourself up and move on!"

Positive self-talk always gave me that shot in the arm. That kick in the pants to get out of the doldrums, whip up a casserole, cheer up a friend, call on another client, or come up with the next latest, greatest, big idea. It would prove to be a lifeline during what was then the worst season of my life.

"I think I can, I think I can," I said, sometimes only half-believing, as I went in for yet another round of chemotherapy. (Those were the days when anti-nausea meds were nothing more than a gleam in some cancer researcher's eye. In the olden days, they gave us the Drano without the feel-better cocktail that today keeps many breast-cancer patients functioning at full throttle during chemo.)

"I think I can, I think I can," I said as I crawled back to bed after throwing up everything but my toenails. For the umpteenth time that day! "I thi-i-nk I can," I sobbed as my hair fell out strand by strand by precious strand. "I think I can" became my mantra as I saw the statistics stacked up to the stratosphere against me.

"Of course you can," I told myself on better days when I felt more like myself. "Because you are *you*! The computer doesn't know you! It doesn't know how much you laugh or cry. Doesn't know how fervently you're prayed for. Doesn't know if you take the pills or flush them! And *duh*! It sure doesn't know that God has a timetable for your life and even for your death. Of course you can!"

"Thought I could," I whispered tenuously at year's end, weakened, not wanting to challenge fate. And chug-chug, puff-puff, I got well.

After that, I thought I had it mastered, this think-I-can religion of mine. That is, until I knelt at the altar of my daughter's breast cancer—and, later, at the grotto of a newly broken and (please, God, no!) lost-forever relationship. The sacrament became harder to observe as life dealt more of its blows. My "pull yourself up by the bootstraps" theology became more and more difficult to preach to others.

Sometimes I couldn't even find my bootstraps.

It took a lot of straws to break this camel's back, but I was all out of self-help techniques. So I began to pray a bit differently. "Lord, I can't do it anymore. But maybe You can."

Then I remembered a verse from Scripture: "Nothing is impossible with God" (Luke 1:37). So I tried every day to turn my broken-down engine over to the greatest Power in the universe. And little by little, I began to relax, letting Him do the chugging and the tugging while I simply went along for the ride.

I've met women (and men) who've been to the edge of hell and back—the pain (whether physical, emotional or both) so severe that they wished themselves dead. At times we sit there on the train tracks of life and are too paralyzed to open our mouths, much less cry out for help. But given enough time, sometimes the very thing that immobilizes us is what teaches our spirit to soar.

Just ask my friend Lois. She's the guru of self-talk . . . and good manners. Lois believes having good manners makes a difference—a difference that plays out in every facet of life from the grades you get in school to the respect you long for in business to whether or not you're invited to that special party. The list goes on!

Lois will tell you in a heartbeat that what you say in your mind (the "I can do its") and how you present yourself to others will give you the self-confidence to meet most—if not all—of life's challenges.

Raised in Aiken, South Carolina, in a home where having good manners was a way of life, Lois credits her parents for having given her the gift of a lifetime—the tools to know how to put the right foot forward to live a positive life. And she's passing (with a boatload of passion!) that know-how to the next generation. As founder and director of the popular etiquette and dining-skills program Your Manners, Lois custom designs classes for children, teens and adults.

"It all started with a tea party," my playful friend will tell you. "I loved it! And before I knew it, I was giving very swanky little-girl tea parties on a regular basis. Complete with fancy hats, gloves and jewelry!"

Observing a few examples of less-than-stellar behavior in her diminutive clientele, Lois saw her niche. She *carped the diem* (which I believe means "seized the fish"). She offered her expertise as a teacher—a *sensei*, if you will—of impeccable manners.

One evening at a grown-up party, a business executive coaxed Lois to tell him about this "etiquette thing" she did. "My sales team needs to meet you," he said.

That encounter led to something Lois never could have predicted. Now she's conducting business- and social-etiquette workshops for adults.

"My phone's ringing off the hook!" she tells me in an email, and she thanks me for giving her pep talks along the way. "They made all the difference," she says.

With or without my pep talks, my cute, blonde girlfriend would have found success. Somehow you can feel the aura around her, and you just *know*: It's Lois's time! Almost as if she's waited her whole life for this moment.

The thing is, Lois has already celebrated her sixtieth birthday. (How long ago, I won't say. Friends don't!) And less than a decade ago, there was a long period when she wanted life to be over. In fact, Lois prayed to die.

I didn't know it when I met her and first heard about her tea parties, but there was a vast disparity between the way Lois felt and how she presented herself.

She made a cheery appearance in her bright green shorts and sunshine-yellow shirt. Her tan was summer-bronze, and she looked as if she'd stepped out of an ad for a Hawaiian golf vacation. Atop her sleek, blonde pageboy, there was perched a large straw hat, laden with decorations—ribbons and bows, golf balls and tees.

I soon found out that beneath the bravado of the hat was a wounded soul. One that lived every day, every hour of life, reliving the reality of her son's suicide. Asking herself, *Why? What could I have done? How can I go on?*

The day I met Lois, I was the guest speaker for The Pat Boone Celebrity Spectacular, an annual golf fundraiser benefiting a Chattanooga children's home that provides a safe haven for children whose parents are in prison.

Celebrities and guests come from all over the country for this event, and while the golfers go off and do, well, whatever it is golfers do, the *womenfolk* have a luncheon that includes a fashion show, a raffle and a speaker. (And yes, my politically correct friend, I did catch a whiff of sexism in the male-female equation of it. But, hey, I was there to be the speaker, not to organize a protest. Let me make this clear: *You don't get paid to protest!*)

When I walked into the hotel dining room for breakfast, my eyes went straight to Lois. Who could miss that big, crazy hat? I couldn't help wondering about the lady under it. So I took my bagel and bacon, pulled up a chair beside her, and we introduced ourselves.

"I have no idea what this is all about," she said with a bewildered shrug. "I only know that I pass this Bethel [the name of the children's home] place every single day, admire the neat campus, and hear bits of news about the good that's done here."

She paused.

Then, almost parenthetically, she added, "My son. Thackston. My son who died. He loved children—just had a natural affinity for them. He would have been a teacher had he lived. So . . . !"

She said it with finality, touching the brim of her hat as though it explained everything. The room grew uncomfortably quiet for a moment.

"I'm so sorry," I said. "How did he die?"

"He took his life," she answered. "But I like to say 'He went to heaven self-invited.'"

Ready to change the subject and feeling the need to explain the bizarre headgear, she said she'd heard about the raffle and wanted to contribute something for the children. Since it was a golf tournament, she had come up with the clever hat idea. She pointed to several more on the raffle table.

I came to understand that Lois was no doubt in the "blue jelly stage" of her tragic experience (in the next chapter I'll explain what I mean by that). She could make hats without much thought. Then, quite unexpectedly, her God-given creativity had kicked in, and the results were more than she'd thought possible.

Later, at the raffle, women practically clawed one another—I'm pretty sure I saw a few well-manicured fingernails broken on the floor—to get to her creations. In the end, the sale of those hats helped raise several hundred dollars for an incredible cause.

Although Lois had planned to drop off her hats and leave, she stayed.

All day she fussed over me and my book table, sat by me at lunch, and helped me pack up afterward. When the day was over, I knew we'd be friends forever. What I didn't know was how many times, as I traveled around speaking and promoting books, I'd find myself parroting Lois's unusual remark.

I'd meet up with another mother whose child had taken his or her own life, or a wife whose husband had died at his own hand (there are more than I could have imagined), and as I fumbled for the right words, I'd inevitably think of Lois. "What you're trying to tell me," I'd say, "is that your child [your loved one] went to heaven self-invited." Then I'd watch a smile come across that person's face as the words of hope and comfort sank in.

Nine years later, very near the anniversary of Thackston's death, Lois and I sat in her pink- and purple-swathed apartment to talk about the journey (one I couldn't have guessed) that had birthed her tea-party career.

"This is what I have left of Thackston," she said, as she pulled a big box into the middle of the living room. We plunked ourselves down beside it. "It's my memories." The fact that the box hadn't been opened since the day she'd packed it away soon after his death awed me to silence.

For the next few hours, we sat on the purple floor and fingered photographs. We cooed over the darling baby that was Thackston, and picture by picture, we watched him grow to manhood.

We giggled at silly little-boy crayon drawings and read out loud awkward, childish poems.

We wolf-whistled at the lifeguard with the toned physique and admired the *GQ*-man in his black tuxedo.

We cried when we came to a letter Lois wrote, which began: "I visited your grave today . . ."

"What do you remember most?" I asked when the last treasure had been examined.

"Hugging him in the kitchen," my friend said, without having to think. "Just reaching up for him and hugging him."

"When the pain got really bad," she explained, "I would think about his love of children, and I'd gather up all the little girls I knew and have a tea party. I even carried a miniature silver tea set and dress-up clothes in the trunk of my car when I went to Florida to visit my sister, just so I could have tea parties on the beach. Not only did it give me great personal joy, but it was also the one thing that made me feel close to my son."

I sat quietly as Lois reflected.

"At each turn of the road," she said, "I was drawn to children, perhaps because I was looking at life through Thackston's eyes. He wanted to spend his life teaching."

"When news came of his death, I was an alien." She shuddered at the thought. "So much so that in my initial grief . . ." She stopped speaking, and the pause was such that I thought she wouldn't be able to go on. ". . . I forgot how to get myself to the bathroom, Sue. Can you believe I couldn't even get myself to the bathroom?" She looked deep into my eyes. "And the mess from it was no more embarrassing to me than it would have been for a newly born infant."

Silence once again filled the room. It seemed that all of Chattanooga was silent for the moment.

"But now!" said my friend. "Now I can see beyond myself—see the good that's come." A tiny smile started in her eyes and then spread across her entire countenance.

"In a way, I've taken on my son's life work." And she gave an unexpected little laugh as the incongruity of it dawned on her.

"Oh, he wouldn't be giving tea parties! But he'd be encouraging children—nourishing their little spirits."

Lois called me soon after I had returned to Nashville to entertain me with the details of a recent tea party and share a remark that was whispered in her ear by one of her protégées.

"You've made me better than I ever dreamed I could be!" said the young girl. It was a defining moment for Lois, and it pretty much sums up what she's all about. Thackston would be proud of his mama!

There *is* power in positive thinking, in self-talk, not only for Lois, but also for others I've met along the way. It's served me well for many years and continues to give me courage to this day.

It is just that, well, there are limits to what pep talks can do. And sometimes we just don't have the energy to give them to ourselves. This is where we need God to come rescue us. Where we declare ourselves powerless on our own, but that with God—*with God!*—all things are possible.

Let *Him* jump start your life again. It's more exciting than the Indy 500! Ladies and gentleman, let *Him* start your engines!

You may not regain the future you had planned for yourself. But often there are wonderful surprises—brought about by the very crisis that stalled your little engine in the first place—that you never could have dreamed or hoped for.

After my "death sentence," I began a new career of writing books and speaking. In other words, what I thought was the end of my life was truly a new beginning.

Dear friend, if you're smothered in crisis, if its boa-constrictor grip has you pinned down and gasping for breath, let me invite you to release the hold by repeating that simple phrase—softly at first, and then with a crescendo: "I think He can. I think He can!"

Therefore, "I think I can, too."
Make it your prayer.

Unleashing Your Inner BHL!

Pick up a copy of *The Little Engine That Could*, even if it's under
the guise of buying it for a child or grandchild. Read it. Carry it
from room to room with you. Prop it up in front of you while
you work. Make its message your own. And do I have to tell
you? Talk to yourself! Tell yourself you can make it. Tell yourself that in spite of *whatever*—and with God's help—one day you'll
be the person you long to be.

A Lame, Lousy Limerick

It's an exercise good for your brain
I learned from a little blue train.
I think I can! You betcha!
The message'll getcha!
Now repeat it once more! Now *again!*

A Pithy, Provocative Quote

*He who would be useful, strong, and happy must
cease to be a passive receptacle for the negative,
beggarly, and impure streams of thought; and as a
wise householder commands his servants and invites
his guests, so must he learn to command his desires
and to say, with authority, what thoughts he shall
admit into the mansion of his soul.*
JAMES ALLEN

CHAPTER 5

Blue Jelly Therapy

Unleashed by Mindless Tasks

Now that you've started talking to yourself, my visual image is you there in your cozy little laundry room, not another person in sight, sorting grubby underwear and socks and begrudgingly slinging static-cling doo-dads—chatting away like you're in your right mind, spouting positive and hopeful platitudes that you don't even believe in your soul of souls . . . but nevertheless, *Sue said!*

And by the way, don't forget that Sue also said, "Invite God to be part of the equation." Though you might not be able to verbalize a prayer of that magnitude while dealing with the mountains of yucky, dirty clothes that have accumulated while you were out of commission, promise you won't forget, okay?

By now I'm hoping you've taken that small step from your bed of blues to the place I'm calling the "blue jelly stage." You're doing something mindless (like laundry!) because if you had a mind, you'd rob a bank and get a maid!

For me, doing things that didn't require brain power was the beginning of my recovery. It didn't take much thought to scrub the kitchen floor. So, soon after my surgery and jump-in-a-hole-and-pull-the-hole-in-with-you diagnosis, I got down on my knees with a bucket of hot, soapy water, against the wishes of everyone around me. Despite their concerns (perhaps legitimate), my body was telling me to *move*.

I once read that in some ancient mystical religion, the followers are taught the value of turning off their busy minds periodically—just to "chop wood and carry water" for a while. I didn't have an axe handy, but I found lots of comfort in sudsy water and the rewards of a clean floor. It was as if my body went on autopilot. I found myself doing things I could do by rote—no brain cells required. This included tidying up spaces that didn't need tidying and cooking food we didn't need either (our meals were graciously being provided by the church).

The only thing I didn't think of making was blue jelly (I'm sure you're wondering about that), which I later discovered was the very thing—the very mindless thing—I should've been doing. Should've because it not only saved another poor soul from despair, but it also made her rich in the process! And it provided her the necessary material for a bestselling book to boot. (And it could've been me! Where in the world was I? Big Lots? For the tenth time that week?)

Allow me to explain.

A year or so ago, when I walked into my niece Sarah's New York City apartment (a block from Central Park, in the same vicinity as Seinfeld's building), I knew it was the perfect place to write. I'd needed to get away and put my nose to the proverbial grindstone on this book, and Sarah needed a sitter for Fish and Eddie while she made a trip to California. (Fish is not a fish, and Eddie isn't a swimmer—though he wears a perfect white-fur bikini on his belly. Fish and Eddie are black cats.)

If I believed in reincarnation (which I don't, but stretch with me here), I'd think I lived my former life in New York City. More than any other place I've been, I feel right at home in the Big Apple. I'm energized by the brouhaha of its masses. Even at night with the windows wide open, the clamor of buses and taxis soothes me to sleep! At home in Nashville, ironically, I'm awakened by the dripping of a faucet.

Contrary to popular belief, I've discovered that "The City" is a friendly place to be. People talk to me. I make them! And as you already know, I talk to myself, so I'm never without company.

How lucky is this? I asked myself, as I set up my laptop (after a long walk in Central Park, of course) and prepared to write. It comforted me to know that, should I not be able to conquer my present state of writer's block, I could avail myself of the myriad books in Sarah's library—a room crammed floor-to-16-foot-ceiling with books, mostly on the art of writing. Which makes sense, since my niece is a big-time author.

At the moment she has a bestselling novel about true love, for which she's sold the movie rights—and she also has a big-bucks (none of your business—well, actually I don't really know) contract for two more books. It would be enough to throw me into fits of jealousy if I didn't love her so much. (Enquiring minds will be interested to know that Michael J. Fox sat at the table right behind me at Sarah's wedding reception at the Boat House in Central Park. I was able to position myself for a photo in such a way that it looked for all the world as though Michael and I were facing each other and chatting intimately. Oh, how I treasure that picture! It's on my dresser.)

Not much writing took place that week in New York. Instead, I found myself devouring—no, make that feasting on!—the treasures around me. I must have fast-read a hundred books, taking notes like a crazy person.

One that grabbed my attention was a tiny volume called *Blue Jelly* by Debby Bull, former editor and writer for *Rolling Stone* magazine. The unlikely subtitle? "Love Lost and the Lessons of Canning." If it's not the best example I've seen of taking a small, mindless step out of despair, I don't know what is!

"I was driven to canning by the wreck of my heart,"[1] Debby writes, and the story that follows, in a nutshell, is this: Girl takes care of boyfriend, puts him through college, keeps house, mows lawn, shops for groceries, cooks, supports him while he writes his book. She even edits his book!

Girl plans big party to celebrate book's completion. Boyfriend calls *after* the guests have arrived to say he won't be there, that he won't ever be there. He's fallen in love with someone else.

Girl is devastated. Her savings are gone. She can't move. She does nothing but sit in front of the tube and watch Court TV. She's in such bad shape that she's jealous of the lucky people who've been murdered by the defendants on trial.

Girl finally musters the strength to clean out the apartment and discovers a bag of blueberries in the freezer. She makes jelly. Next she pickles the vegetables from boyfriend's abandoned garden and coincidentally happens to find her grandmother's blue Ball jars, which she feels compelled to fill. When blue Ball jars cover the countertops, our gal knows she can live through her crisis.

In the words of the author: "Canning may sound like a strange path out of the dark woods of despair, but all other ways, from Prozac to suicide, are really hard on your body. When you're depressed you have to do something that takes you out of the drama that makes you detach from the big world and become queen of a tiny, controllable world, like one of berries and Ball jars."[2]

I put the book down and experienced the sort of epiphany that comes with a delayed understanding of some past experience. I realized that taking baby steps—mindlessly scrubbing floors—allowed me to shuffle on toward healing. Each small task I completed gave me the courage to take even bigger steps. It was the emotional vehicle that empowered me to edge my way back to my Big-Haired world. Losing a breast may seem like a minor tribulation (especially compared to the alternative, losing my life!)—nevertheless, this double-D-sized loss nearly paralyzed me.

Needless to say, finding out everything I could find out about reconstructive surgery became a top priority. And may I just say, miracles are happening every day in the world of plastic surgery—and I, for one, give thanks daily. Who would have thought it possible to tunnel my tummy fat up through my midriff (along with some muscle and blood supply) to rebuild the body parts I was grieving. Who would have thought I'd be happier with my body after surgery than I was before? Talk about a bonus! Talk about Barbie-doll boobs!

Forcing myself to get out of bed, get dressed, scrub floors and cook gave me a safe, simple backdrop against which I could start to ponder my future. Little by little, I began to face the grim fact that had my doctors taken my complaints seriously, I would have been diagnosed two years earlier. How deeply I resented the fact that I might have avoided this trauma to psyche, soul and body, had they just *listened to me* and followed up with testing, rather than patting me on the hand and assuring me that all was well.

The angrier I got, the harder I slung that mop! My floors were never cleaner. And my family was threatening to borrow some of those big, yellow plastic cones from Wal-Mart—the kind they use to block the entrance to the restroom every time I need to use it—if I didn't stop.

But over time, mundane, going-through-the-motions tasks like mopping the floor helped me gradually let go of some of my pent-up rage. Each day I made a teensy bit of progress. And soon I was able to trust myself to go the next mental level, which was to calmly weigh the facts of my disease against all the available alternatives and commit to a course of treatment with a clear head.

Eventually I was brave enough to boldly shake my fist in the face of cancer and say (you've heard it before and you'll hear it again before I'm through): "I'm nobody's statistic!"

Over and over I reminded myself that the computer doesn't know me. It doesn't know how much I laugh or cry, doesn't know what I eat and drink, how much sleep I get or whether or not I make healthy choices. It isn't aware that I am the only—the very only—Suzanne Davis Buchanan, who comes from a long line of sturdy progenitors: Most of those Davises, Entsmingers, McKnights, Nelsons and Braleys lived long, healthy lives, and so will I! There are a million, maybe a trillion, other minuscule things that the Big Life-or-Death Calculator can never take into consideration. It can't know that I'm wrapped in the loving care of family and friends, that I'm prayed for, that God has a timetable for my life and for my death. Furthermore, I doubt there will ever be a computer invented that can know whether I'll take my prescribed medications or flush them down the toilet.

Here's what I'm getting at: I experienced an overwhelming attitude adjustment. Not only did I move from helpless to hopeful, but I was ready to pick a fight with anyone who got in the way of my recovery.

Perhaps what I'm proposing here seems too simple. But then I told you early on, I'm not a psychologist or a scientist! I'm a strive-to-figure-it-out kind of person. For me, the best solutions have always been simple ones.

What is your crisis? What tempts you to duck under the bedcovers and hide? A health problem? A kid gone wrong? A marriage that's crumbling before your disbelieving eyes? Or is it something less traumatic, like a stack of bills you're avoiding or that dreaded phone call you need to make to a friend, relative or potential boss?

Let me invite you to get out of bed, put one foot on the floor, then the other, and go throw in a load of wash—pausing to remember the ancient saying, "Before enlightenment, comes the laundry."

Maybe you'll head for the garage and overhaul an engine, or if you aren't the coveralls type, tie on your apron and take on the kitchen. Make scratch brownies or fry chicken the old-fashioned way. Maybe you'll eventually make a fortune, like our friend the jelly maker or my adorable, been-through-the-crisis, tight-fittin'-jeans-wearin', motorcycle-ridin' friend Anne of Auntie Anne's Pretzels. Do something tactile that doesn't mentally tire you—something with a definite finish line in sight. You'll be glad you did.

Come on! Trust me! It will work. Visualize yourself leaning on me, a fellow survivor, as you take the difficult first steps. Every step after will be easier.

If you're still stuck to the mattress because it's necessary for your recovery, ask someone who loves you to glue some of those luminous stars on your bedroom ceiling. Then, when you're discouraged, lie back on your pillow and reach for them. It won't be long till you're out of the dumps and touching heaven again. *Really!*

Eventually, that small effort will lead you, step by step, to a Technicolor life of empowerment and fulfillment you could not have imagined.

Unleashing Your Inner BHL!

Wow! I can't believe I said that: Glue some of those luminous stars on your bedroom ceiling. What a great idea, if I do say so myself. (You can get all sorts of fun stuff to stick on the ceiling at your local teachers' supply store!)

Everybody has a shelf full of cookbooks (most of them covered with beautiful pictures of food and a nice sprinkling of dust). Perhaps the time has come to pull out those books, find a few interesting recipes and get to work.

If you really want to get inspired, turn on one of those great cooking shows, like the one with Rachael Ray (who, by the way,

I'm praying for—that she'll settle in as she gets older and slow down so I can keep up. Lasagna in 20 minutes? I don't think so.). I'd also highly recommend that southern talkin' Paula Dean, who has a motorcycle-riding honey of a boyfriend and believes in recipes with real, honest-to-goodness butter. And that wild-eyed, crazy cook "Kick it up a notch!" Emeril is good for an idea or two.

Most large cities have cooking classes, where you just sit and eat while the chefs do the work. That's *my* kind of cooking.

I'll try it if you will!

A Lame, Lousy Limerick

You've had more than your share, but *shazam!*
Don't just sit there and pout! No, ma'am!
Take to your kitchen,
And stop all that . . . (whoops!) complaining
Like the girl who made jelly and jam!

A Pithy, Provocative Quote

*Mindless activities keep you going until your
brain fires up or your heart is mended . . .
whichever comes first!*
BECKY JOHNSON

Notes
1. Debby Bull, *Blue Jelly* (New York: Hyperion Books, 1997), p. 3.
2. Ibid., pp. 5-6.

CHAPTER 6

Never Let the Truth Get in the Way of a Good Story!

Unleashing Your History (Embellishments Encouraged)

Is there something that's still holding you back? As in "I could be unleashed to greatness, cuteness, wit or whatever . . . *but!*"?

My guess is maybe you've been held back by your past.

Perhaps what controls you most right now is what you've done or not done in life. You're embarrassed. You didn't have the advantages others had. You were poor, you were dumb, you flunked out. Or maybe you failed at school, at marriage, at motherhood. You were abused, popped pills, smoked dope, shot up, aborted. You could boil it all down to this: You've made bad decisions and have missed opportunities.

Or maybe you've done everything right . . . *but!* You're easily intimidated, hate the way you look, think you can't hold your own in a conversation, have a poor self-image, feel generally inept.

You know the script.

But like it or not, you are your story! Everything that's happened in your life—the good, the bad and the ugly—has made *you* who you are today.

To tell you the truth (and I'd walk on my lips before I'd tell you a lie), it's not just the events of your history that make you who you are. It's your *version* of your history that counts, and it's your prerogative to add new purpose to old pain or change the lens through which you view the past. In the story you've attached yourself to, you can be a victim or a victor. You can be "poor and homeless," or you can boast about your "unusual, interesting and bohemian" family.

Think it can't be done? Just go to Amazon.com and order *The Glass Castle*, a memoir by Jeannette Hunt. It's a fabulous read and the perfect example of what I'm talking about. The author describes a crazy life with nomadic, poverty-stricken parents who on the one hand got drunk, stole and betrayed their children by leaving them alone for weeks at a time to fend for themselves, and on the other hand gave them unconditional love, captured their imaginations and taught them to embrace life fearlessly. Jeannette credits her parents for giving her the hope and determination to become the successful person she is today.

With a few decades of experiences behind me, it's my not-so-humble opinion that you may as well laugh at yourself, dear reader. Cancel your appointment with the therapist and save the money for important things in life, like shoes, purses and Victoria's Secret!

Once you come to grips with your history and realize that no matter how hard you try, you can never change what happened, then you can accept it and move on. Even better, you can take a fresh look in your rearview mirror and, with God's help, see a new story—one that's redemptive, perhaps even empowering. Then plant those gorgeous, new faux-Pradas firmly in *today* and *tomorrow*, which is your reality.

Beating yourself up over your past isn't only unproductive; it makes you ugly. *Dog-breath ugly!* And I'd rather age with contentment and peace than turn old, ugly and bitter by hanging onto past pain. My motto? "Lookin' good is half the battle."

I am my story. And it's a good one, if I do say so myself!

Let me start at the very beginning . . .

My father was a brave, brave warrior and my mother was an Indian princess. We lived in an idyllic Green-Giant kind of valley, with wild animals as friends and . . .

Okay, okay! That's not true. But if there's one thing I learned long ago, it's to never let the truth get in the way of a good story.

A good story! That pretty much sums up my childhood. If there were problems (and I'm sure there were), I was, for the most part, oblivious to them. We lived in a little white cottage with a front porch that had a swing and a glider. Daddy had a good job, and Mama wore starched, nipped-in-at-the-waist house dresses and high-heeled shoes—and she sang along with Kate Smith when she ironed our clothes.

Mother cooked wonderful meals every night and made pies with meringue piled up to heaven. Our cousins lived across the street, and we could walk a block to the Methodist Church (that to this day has a stained-glass window with our family name on it) and to Jolly's Market around the corner.

Yes, I am my story. Even today I'm just a continuation of the little Pollyanna from West Virginia who lived her life only to have fun.

Early on, I called myself Mrs. Vandertweezers and dressed in my mama's cast-off satin blouse, which dragged the floor. On my feet were high-heeled shoes that let my toes poke out. On my head, a big hat with a veil down to *there*. And everywhere else, an overabundance of glittery jewelry, compliments of my Aunt Ginny. Sometimes Mrs. Vandertweezers's mother would give in to a little makeup, and when she turned her back, it was applied in great gobs. Around Mrs. V's neck was the ultimate accessory, the final touch, the *pièce de résistance*: a furry animal that bit its own tail.

Mrs. Vandertweezers dressed her cat (Smokey the Pirate Don Derk of Don Day) in doll clothes, laid him on his back in the baby buggy and off they went up the street. Past the convent, past the Catholic school, past the Catholic church, to the corner (which was as far as she was allowed to go) and back again. Mrs. V lived only to be known and noticed by the neighbors on her block—and believe me, she was!

Today, she's that same little girl. It's just that her neighborhood has gotten bigger.

We *did* live in a valley: the Kanawha Valley, Charleston, West Virginia, known as "the chemical valley," full of pollution-spewing smoke stacks from the likes of Union Carbide, Monsanto, WestVaco and DuPont. Some claimed we were on the top-ten list of places where, should war break out, "the bomb" (I knew about "the bomb" from eavesdropping on the adults) would be dropped. That would cause the rest of the country to shut down automatically because it took chemicals to run the nation. We'd be blasted to smithereens and back. *Why, oh why, God, couldn't we live in Ohio on a farm?* I wondered and worried. (A farm in Ohio was the most faraway place I could imagine, since that's where my grandparents lived—I'd never been anywhere else.)

Occasionally there'd be an explosion at one of the chemical plants, and folks would be killed. Our house would shake so hard our teeth would rattle. Then no one would say a word; we'd just hold our breath and wait for smithereens. We wouldn't know what had happened until hours later, when we'd chase down the paper boy who made his way from corner to corner, shouting, "Extra! Extra! Read all about it!"

We didn't have television. The first time I ever saw TV was when I was a tiny girl and we were invited to someone's house to watch Princess Elizabeth's wedding. In black and white, and so fuzzy you could barely make out the images, the broadcast was still impressive enough for me to organize neighborhood royal weddings for years to come.

As Mrs. Vandertweezers, I married someone I called "Manny." Not long ago, I was told by a lady who knew me then, who had worked for my father in a department store, that I had talked of "Manny" until I was quite "a long-legged kid." (Translation: till I was much too old to have an imaginary husband!)

This old friend of my parents said that one day I came into the store with my mother and was asked about Manny's well-being. She reported that a strange look came over my face, that I paused for a moment before answering, "He died." Try as they did, they could never get me to speak of Manny again.

So now you know. I spent my childhood living in a make-believe world with an imaginary husband—named Manny, no less!—fearing a bomb that never came and mooning over a coronation that wasn't much more than a tourist attraction.

As the country song says, "That's my story, and I'm stickin' to it."[1]

So, what's your story? If you tell me your childhood was uneventful, uninteresting or boring, lean close and listen to my word of advice, dear reader: *Exaggerate!* As a Southern-bred, full-of-laughs friend of mine says, "We were as dysfunctional as the next family, but at least we had the decency to make it sound entertaining."

Some of you don't have to exaggerate. Some of you have stories that are beyond belief! Abuse is rampant everywhere I go—physical, sexual and mental abuse. Whenever I hear stories from women who've experienced this unspeakable trauma, I get angry. Angry enough to kill! I'm tired of hearing the word "forgive" roll off the tongue so easily.

Forgiveness is possible, but anger should not be a forbidden word or a negated emotion. You cannot heal what you cannot feel.

Let me say that again: *You cannot heal what you cannot feel.*

So it's healthy and necessary for part of your past to include honesty about your pain; honesty about the anger that followed; and hopefully, honesty about how you finally spoke the truth, called a spade a spade, and went through whatever process it took to heal and come out a victor, not a victim. Recovery, success, happiness and generosity are the best revenge, and they make a wonderful end-cap to a story that got bogged down somewhere in a pit of pain.

In your mind's eye, picture a fine painting. Something from the era of the Old Masters. Think Monet, Renoir, Degas, Rembrandt, Raphael. If you can't recall, pick up an art book or go online. What colors stand out in your mind's eye? Red, yellow, orange, fuchsia, magenta, green, blue! And every shade in between. Those are the colors that catch your eye and stay in your memory.

Now look again.

Did you happen to notice the dark areas? The heavy shadings of brown, black and gray that seem to have been created with an angry slash of the brush? Without those dark places, there would be no true beauty. The painting would have no depth, no dimension. It wouldn't even qualify as cheap, motel-room art!

It's the same with you and me. It takes the dark places to bring out the color and beauty of the finished work.

I'm thankful for those sweet, safe years of childhood. I had no reason to think life would be otherwise. But guess what? It was . . .

Unleashing Your Inner BHL!

Life is full of joy and woe. Some people find they are helped by writing two versions of their life story: one in which they are the victim, and the other in which they come out the victorious hero!

Here's what I suggest for you: Start by remembering and writing down (perhaps even adding photos to) the good memories.

Write about the people you cherished. The animals you loved. The vacations you took. What made you laugh? What embarrassed you at the time but now makes you laugh? (I've got plenty of those!) Write about peaceful moments.

Later, you can pick up the brush and palette, and paint in the dark places—the shadings that represent pain and sadness. Those will complete the picture and make it more authentic.

If, after all this, your story still bores you, well, you have my permission to "decorate it"! Embellish your past until it zings and sings the way you want it to. Call it a novel, if you must! Who knows? The Big-Haired Lady inside you may just decide to take a few writing lessons, get a professional editor and sell it to a New York publisher.

Tell you what. I'll come to your first book signing! Call me!

A Lame, Lousy Limerick

She wore jewels, a fur cape and a hat
Strolled the street all dressed up, with her cat.
Little did she know,
And it came as a blow
To learn life would be nothing like *that*!

A Pithy, Provocative Quote

Every woman has a story to tell, and every woman has a story to hear. Sometimes we tell, and sometimes we listen.

JANICE CHAFFEE

Note

1. Jimmy Buffet, "That's My Story and I'm Stickin' to It," © Jay Oliver Music, New York, NY.

CHAPTER 7

When It Rains, It Pours (and Other Soggy Truths)

Unleashing the Rest of the Story

"Why me?"

That's the question most folks ask when they've been hit head-on by a freight-train-going-at-full-speed kind of crisis. It's only natural.

Why do I have breast cancer? Why is my child disabled? Why was I deserted? Why was I abused? Why am I bankrupt? Why did my wife leave me for another man? Why did my loved one take his own life? Why me? Why my loved ones?

My question was, *Why are so many bad things happening all at once?* Thanks to cancer and chemo, I'd lost my identity. My breasts, my skin tone, my hair and my eyebrows were gone, and let's see . . . how do I say this? I no longer needed a bikini wax! On top of that, I had to face the prognosis and probable outcome of my diagnosis. And it didn't look too hopeful. (A "friend" told my daughter, "Your mother's as good as gone!" That girl shoulda been *shut-yer-mouth* tarred 'n' feathered!)

I had to cope with the ravages of the disease, which included being deathly sick and having hallucinations caused by a reaction to the medicine. Discovering my doctor's notes, which said I'd be dead before the end of the year, didn't help either.

Added to that, I was watching my mother wither away to nothing from the same ugly cancer that was running rampant in me. I was forced to deal with her difficult and controlling husband, who forbade her to have chemotherapy, saying, "If it makes you that sick, it can't be good for you."

Choosing my mother's casket, deciding on the clothes she'd be laid out in and planning her funeral felt like a prelude to my own. I was certain I'd be next.

"When it rains, it pours!"

Noah's wife said that. It was the thirty-ninth day she'd been on that creaky ark with all those sneezing, sniveling relatives. Everyone was out of clothes; the ones she'd washed five days earlier were still wet, and they were going through the food supply faster than she'd ever thought possible. She was fed up with fur balls, and she'd had all she could stand of those restless, smelly, wet animals. She didn't dare turn her back for fear of being kicked by a kangaroo, swatted by a lion or stepped on by a rhinoceros. She'd been a reasonably healthy woman when she stepped on that boat. Now she was pneumonic, claustrophobic and paranoid, with a permanent case of seasickness to boot.

"When it rains, it pours!" Noah's wife never realized it, but her words caught on like loincloths after the Fall of Man, and all through history, people have repeated it.

Sarah said it to Abraham: "Abraham, it seems to me that when it rains, it pours. Does it seem that way to you?"

And Lot said to Lot's wife: "Wife, did you ever notice? When it rains, it pours!"

Even Napoleon, at the Battle of Waterloo, surely leaned over to his trusty field marshal and said, "Monsieur Fieeeld Marshalle! When eeet rains, eeeet pours, non?"

Down through the ages, when the load became almost too heavy to bear—when everything bad seemed to happen at once—

folks have quoted Mrs. Noah. Her slogan was so catchy, so popular, it was eventually picked up by a salt company!

"If it were just cancer (or divorce, or bankruptcy) I could handle it," I've heard over and over, "but all these other things are happening at the same time." When it comes to problems, they really
do seem to come in torrents, and this was certainly true for me.

That's when I began to journal.

Never in those cutesy, little blank books (they are more pro-
lific than books on friendship) that are found everywhere from
drug stores to airports to Bloomingdales. It never occurred to
me that my thoughts (not to mention my penmanship) were
worthy of those store-bought books. Nope. My notes are always
written on envelopes, napkins, church bulletins and airplane
tickets—whatever is handy. The two-drawer nightstand on my
side of the bed was and is to this very day stuffed full of my
middle-of-the-night ruminations.

Eventually, assuming I can read what I've written, I transfer
them to my computer and organize them. Those early "chicken
scratchings" became my first book. (Though there are still a few
I can't quite make sense of, notes like, "All I want in life is an
island to myself and some cute, young cabana boy to wait on
me" and "Forget therapy. It's too expensive. Poppin' bubble
wrap is cheap and probably works just as good." There's another one stuck to the back of the bubble wrap one and I can't quite
make it out. But it has to do with nudity.)

There were days when I was overwhelmed by my huggermug-
gers (look it up in the unabridged, girlfriend) and times when the
chemotherapy played games with my mind. Often I couldn't
think logically. When I did have lucid thoughts, I began to write
them down. I didn't call it journaling back then. In fact, I still don't.
I called it "keeping track." I just wrote because I felt better afterward.

As the compelling need to record my story took over, I began
to think of my writing as a way of speaking to my children.

At some future date when I wouldn't be around, I wanted them to know me. To pick up my journal and understand how I had managed to survive this difficult time. To know I was the same person I had been before the disease. To know I was funny, that I knew how to celebrate, that I was compassionate and that I valued my friendships. I longed for them to understand their place in the scheme of things and that I had found redemption in my story. I pictured a long line of progenitors reading my words, just as I had read about my own ancestors the night of my mother's funeral when I discovered a treasure trove of old letters. They would weep for me as I had wept.

Long after the cancer was gone, I wrote. Rarely was it when circumstances were good, but rather when woes were choking the very breath from me. I wrote because I was brokenhearted. I wrote because relationships had been turned upside down. I wrote when I felt alone, when I felt no one was listening.

Sometimes I'd go back and reread what I'd written, and it was gobble-de-gook. Other times, it was so profound it was mind-boggling! Occasionally it was poetry—poetry I wasn't capable of writing under normal circumstances.

One example is a poem I wrote when I was alienated from my younger daughter. The whys and wherefores aren't mine to tell, but I have permission to say this much as background. Melinda, who was homecoming princess and voted "most talented" in her private high school, made some bad decisions (eight years' worth) that affected us all. This birthday poem was written from the depth of my despair.

A Mother's Heart
(On your birthday)

There is a place within my heart
That holds you closer now than when

I was your only hope for life.
I love you more than I did then.

The celebration of each day
Has been brought down by anguished soul
That seeks to find and then to fill
The gaping, empty, hateful hole.

What is the cause? What is so wrong?
By night I wonder as I toss.
I want to die to gain relief
To rid my soul from ache of loss.

The loss is us. It's you and me!
Your touch! Your smell! My child conceived.
The hurt within me knows no bounds,
To know we lost the life we weaved.

We've lost the hours, the days and years
But more than this, the thing I find
(It's almost more than I can bear),
I've lost the knowing of your mind.

There is a place within my heart
That holds you closer now than when
I was your only hope for life.
I love you more than I did then.

Now, I'm happy to report, Mindy is once again part of the
family. She calls and drops by often, rarely coming empty-
handed, and her gifts are always unique—something only she
would think of. I tell her she has the "gift of gift-giving." She has

a darling apartment, a shiny car and two show-quality cats she loves dearly. She's a reliable and loyal employee, and she holds down an extra job to make ends meet.

One day I asked, "What changed? What turned you around?" Her answer was profound.

"Mama," she said, "I just got sick of myself."

We'd all be better people if we only got sick of ourselves and changed the things that devour our energies and damage our relationships.

Our older daughter, Dana, was diagnosed with breast cancer seven years ago and went through chemotherapy. She's a harpist and a writer, and she lives in Ohio with her husband, Barry, and their cat, Puddin'.

All I can tell you about watching my daughters navigate life-shaking crises is that a lump in your throat is worse than a lump in your breast. It's a million times harder to go through things with your children than it is to go through them yourself.

The pain and suffering we're dealt in life is often hard to make sense of. But my friend Peggy has a simple suggestion for sorting it out. "Take a blank piece of paper and make two columns," she says. "In one column, list the Good Things, and in the other, the Bad Things." Peggy promises if you wait long enough, many of the things you thought of as bad will jump across the page to the good column. I can guaran-darn-tee you it's been true for me and true for those I love, too.

Would I wish heartache for my daughters? Never in a million years!

But would I wish them to become the women they are today—women with a fuller understanding of life, a greater capacity to appreciate it and a genuine empathy for those around them? The answer is yes.

Everyone's pain is different, and mine is nothing compared to that of others who've been damaged at the hand of someone who claimed to love them. Meet my new friend, a brown-haired, snappy-eyed mother of two. Picture us in a rustic retreat setting, where I've been the speaker for a church conference. I'm sitting on the steps of an old staircase, and she's draped over the banister, half standing, half hanging there. As she tells me her story, her fingers are clenched around the knob on the old newel post.

"He abused my children!" Her voice sounds hollow and hopeless. "I didn't even guess it was happening. He's gone now, and I know I have to forgive—and show my kids how to forgive. But it's not easy. I guess you could say I'm in the process."

Her merciless grip on the antique wooden knob says otherwise. It's almost as though her hands hold the very throat of her vicious offender. Suddenly, a look of guilt flashes across her face—there and gone like the flash of a camera. She wilts. Her hands go limp. She repeats herself, "I have to forgive. And the kids have to forgive! How do I get it through their heads? Through my own head?" she asks.

Dear reader, I'm not a counselor and don't pretend to be. I'm a listener, a cheerleader at best. But that day on that stairway, I heard myself shouting in her face: "No! Stop talking forgiveness. It's too soon—too raw! You have a right to be angry. Your kids need to see you put your fist through the wall. See you go crazy, for their sake if nothing else! Forgiveness is somewhere beyond that, though I'm not sure where. But please, go home and validate their experience and show them the truth. Healing and forgiveness can't happen until you do."

Your story may be one of abuse. If so, you need to get pretty . . . umm . . . *umm* . . . *darn* mad! Stick your fist through the wall! Kick the door down! Go crazy! Validate what has happened. It's only then healing can begin.

Perhaps you've experienced a death—or another tragedy that happened through no fault of your own. Get your story out there, where you can make sense of it.

It'll be tough at first. If you're writing your story, you may one day want to delete some of what you've written. I had to do that in the case of my mother's husband. First of all, I didn't want to think about him again and again. And second, he didn't deserve to be included in our family history. Delete, delete, delete.

With all my heart, dear, precious reader, I encourage you to embrace "the rest of the story." The story you hadn't intended to admit to, either because it's too embarrassing or too painful—or both. Perhaps bringing it out in the open will let you make sense of what's happened to you. Perhaps your thinking is off base, and the observations of another wise person (a counselor or even a girlfriend who's been there, done that) can offer a new perspective.

Is there unfinished business you need to deal with? If so, pray over the issues and ask God how He might have you finish this chapter in a way that is honest. Ask Him to turn your wounds into a place where compassion for others can grow.

Come on, my friend! Take this healing step for your own sanity. Sort it all out, and maybe, just maybe, in the sorting you'll discover wonderful truths.

Perhaps just the *doing* of it will turn into an adventure. Perhaps you'll be able to record a legacy that will comfort and give courage to a future generation. Maybe not now—maybe not even next week—but eventually you'll dig deep enough to find the adventuresome, fun-loving, possibly-even-big-haired *you* you've been looking for.

Unleashing Your Inner BHL!

You may need a counselor or at least a friend who is a good listener. You may need medication to help you find freedom from the pain. Don't hesitate. Tell someone your story; deal with the pain in your past. It's a part of your history that can't be erased, no matter how badly you wish you could do just that.

Write for dear life! Do it for you—on yellow pads or sticky notes or in one of those cutesy diaries if you must. Do it in bits, pieces and chunks, catch-as-catch-can, as I did.

If poetry is your thing, write in rhyme—or let loose in one continuous stream of consciousness. If you use the computer, turn off the screen and forget about format, punctuation and grammar. You can always fix it later or push "delete."

If you don't type or don't like to write, talk into a recorder. But before you begin, fling that feather boa around your spirit. It's a sign that you're searching for *you*!

And don't forget Peggy's idea: Make two columns, and list the Good Things in one and the Bad Things in the other. Wait awhile, and watch what happens!

A Lame, Lousy Limerick

You are your story; your story is you
Come to your senses; it's long overdue
I think you can face it,
And maybe embrace it
Get a grip and face life anew!

A Pithy, Provocative Quote

Don't ask what the world needs. Ask what makes you come alive, for the world needs more people who are fully alive.
JOHN ELDRIDGE

CHAPTER 8

If All Is Not Lost, then Where Did It Go?

Unleashing Yourself to Grieve for Those Around You

Years ago on a visit to Greece, my husband, Wayne, and I noticed that the old ladies were dressed from head to toe in loosely fitting, droopy black clothing. Each one walked as if the weight of the world were on her shoulders. Our guide explained that as young women, these Greek ladies donned black only in times of mourning and that the customary grieving period lasted six months. But as time went by—and as more and more losses occurred, with each episode of mourning overflowing into the next—they simply came to accept their black garb as a way of life. Grief began to permeate and finally consume their lives.

Perhaps Job of the Old Testament knew more about grief than anyone.

"What I feared has come upon me," Job cried (see 3:25). "What I dreaded has happened to me. *Oy vey!*" (The *Oy vey* is mine, but it stands to reason that's what he said, being Jewish for goodness sake! The phrase is a Yiddish exclamation of pain or grief that means "Woe is me.")

My problem is that the things I feared happened—and the things I never thought would happen did too! *Oy vey!*

I've found that there are a lot of *Oy veys*—in-your-face losses—that come to pass simply because life happens. The job that was lost, the house that burned, the friend who was disloyal, the accident, the divorce. Many *Oy veys* are out of our control; they're created by the bad choices or mean-spiritedness of others. (For example, the grief suffered by grandparents who, following their child's messy divorce, are not allowed to see their grandchildren.)

My heart hurts for those who mourn alone. Perhaps it's the wife who's paralyzed by fear because of an abusive spouse—the husband who's charming in public but keeps her "in her place" with cruel words at home. The mistreated children. The marriage that's nothing more than a facade. The spouse who would never dream of being unfaithful but who winces when he touches you. Is this not perhaps grief of the worst kind?

Grief accumulates. It's like the skin of an onion—layer after layer after layer, it accumulates.

My precious friend Lois's sorrow for her son, Thackston, barely began the day he died. Now, years later, she mourns more than ever. The "what ifs." The camaraderie she's missed. The fun that should have been theirs for a lifetime. The Christmases, Thanksgivings, birthdays, vacations. The toasts on New Year's Eve. And how her body aches for that one thing she can't get out of her mind: standing in the kitchen together, hugging.

Layer after layer after layer, the grief piles up.

My friend Peggy huddled with her friends (I among them) at her son Tom's grave, and we mourned as though our hearts would break. We sent flowers and cards, and we comforted Peg as best we could with phone calls and dinners and movies— mere distractions!

Years later, Peggy glimpses Tom's image in the face of one of his children, and it jolts her to the core. Tears fall at the mere sight of a garden because that's the place where she and Tom spent time together, working the soil. Oh, to create just one more garden with her beloved boy!

Time moves on—days become weeks, weeks become months, months become years. Like the layers of an onion . . . layer upon layer upon layer.

We shared, as best we could, overwhelming and mind-numbing grief with our friends Ed and Jan as they laid to rest their beautiful daughter, Ashley. After the funeral, we somehow busied ourselves with life, while Ed and Jan had to deal with the reality of sorting through her treasures and dealing with their lost dreams . . . one by one by one . . . gone! There would be no leather-bound wedding album. No soft-focus memories of a stunning Ashley in her white bridal gown. Posing with her mama. Giggling with her daddy. Bridesmaids sheathed in fairytale dresses. Ashley's three proud brothers, grinning for dear life, rosebuds placed just-so in the lapels of their black tuxedos. Smiling . . . smiling.

Layer after layer after layer, grief accumulates.

We go to a rather large church, and to keep us connected, we are divided into small fellowship groups. Ours meets on Sunday night, and because most of us have been together since the invention of dirt, we're like family. We like nothing better than to get together to eat and laugh and—if we don't get too carried away in our frivolity—pray for one another. Too many times to count, our praying has taken place in a hospital waiting room or an emergency room. And we're all too familiar with funeral homes as well.

Our lives were drastically changed when our friends David and Nancy gave birth to a baby girl who suffered from a rare genetic disorder for which there's no cure. They named her Hope.

On the outside, Hope was perfect and beautiful in every way, and for a while it was hard for us to get it through our heads that something was wrong—that inside that lovely little shell of a body, nothing was as it should have been. Death, it seemed, was programmed into her every cell. They told us that from the moment of her birth the systems inside her had already begun shutting down. Hope couldn't see or hear or swallow food.

But for six months we celebrated her life. Oh, how we celebrated! She was passed around, cooed over, sung to and even
fought over. We bought Teddy bears and dolls and cute little
outfits, and we dressed her up and took a thousand pictures.
She even had her own website! We called her "our" baby.

Nancy and David threw parties for her—extravagant, joyful
parties!—weekly and monthly birthday parties to make up for
the ones that would be missing in the years to come.

Sometimes a knowing look or a smile would cross Hope's
face, and we'd all gather 'round and agree—insist, really!—that
she could see and hear us. That she got it! If only for a moment,
she *knew*!

"And if not," someone would eagerly point out, "she'll know
when she gets to heaven. She'll remember it all!"

After six months, we ushered our precious baby girl into the
presence of God.

Then, against all odds and after a medical procedure to
eliminate the possibility of another pregnancy, Nancy gave birth
to a second child who had the same disease. This time it was a
little boy they named Gabriel. Again we celebrated. Once again
we cooed over, sang to, fought over and took pictures with "our"
precious baby, and his parents gave extravagant and joyful
birthday parties.

Never for a moment did we doubt that Gabriel was a magnificent and treasured gift sent from the Father in heaven.

Sometimes, just as with Hope, a knowing look would cross
Gabe's sweet face, and he'd smile that funny little smile. And
we'd all gather 'round and agree—insist, really—that he knew! If
only for a moment, *he knew!*

"And if not," we'd comfort ourselves, "he'll know when he
gets to heaven. He'll remember it all!"

Six months later, almost to the day of his birth, we gathered
on a familiar hillside and buried him next to his sister.

Nancy wrote in her journal on the New Year's Eve after Hope's death: "All the best, most enjoyable moments for our family are tinged with the fact that she isn't here. We're not complete. And I suppose that goes on forever."

Grief accumulates for the Guthries. As it does for us all.[1]

Once while speaking in Grand Rapids, Michigan, I met several young mothers of disabled children. Eager to understand the burden they carry (these women often get lost in the shuffle), I suggested we find a time they could join me at the beautiful Amway Grand Hotel where they could not only enjoy the luxury of the hotel, but we could get to know each other.

After a satisfying dinner by a warm, cozy fire in the hotel restaurant, we got into our jammies and made ourselves comfy on big four-poster beds in the opulent suite. "So, what's it like?" I asked. "Share some of your struggles and joys with me."

I didn't have to say another word for hours. Sometimes the stories were heart-wrenching, like the time one of them called her pastor in total desperation, in the midst of a life-or-death situation, and he put her on hold. But most were off-the-charts joyous, and I was struck by how many unexpected blessings come with a disabled child. Over and over they assured me that the pluses outweighed the minuses.

I'm not sure if I was invited or if I invited myself to go home with them, but somehow that's exactly what happened. I spent a day with each family, seeing firsthand what it was like. And oh my, I could write a book! (Wait. I *am* writing a book!)

Joy and contentment reigned supreme in each household. Was it difficult? And were there deep concerns? You betcha! The ever-present, unspoken question was, *What next? When will there be another crisis—another middle-of-the-night visit to the emergency room? (Another pastor who puts you on hold?)* In many ways it seems these mothers are never quite able to put their full weight down. They're always on guard. The wear and tear on the body and mind is mind-boggling, as is the enormity of the financial burden.

I spent the night with Candy and her family, and we've become great email friends. Her son Trent was born nearly deaf and with a condition that threatens his breathing and therefore his life. At Candy's house, however, I became an instant believer that the positives outweigh the negatives. I wanted to move in with them! Trent is a fabulous little boy, and when he isn't participating in the activities of the other kids in the family, he's their most enthusiastic cheerleader.

Candy is quick to mention the lessons learned from having a child like Trent. Her 13-year-old daughter dreamed of being president until her brother was born. Now she hopes to teach special needs children. Why? "Because," she explains, "my little brother Trent has taught me to appreciate the little things in life and to pursue life with a passion."

Yet there's an undeniable, ongoing sadness for Candy and Dave when they watch Trent sit on the sidelines, struggling for his breath, and wonder when he might be taken from them.

Grief comes at us in many ways, and it accumulates. But according to my friends, "the good usually outweighs the bad."

Then there are lesser losses, some we're embarrassed to admit. They seem so trite! For instance, the loss of our youth. We feel it with each passing year. Sure, having cancer, losing a child to drugs, or going through divorce or abuse is a thousand times worse than growing older. But it's another layer in the emotional accumulation of *stuff*.

For me, revisiting my old neighborhood and examining the signposts of my childhood bring a gut-sucking emotion very much like . . . what? Grief, perhaps? I miss that my parents aren't sitting there on the porch swing, hugging. No couple ever did more hugging than my folks! I miss the hastily drawn hopscotch grids that used to line the walkway. The games of hide-and-seek in the lumberyard till long after dark. I miss those early friendships. It seems like only yesterday!

I see the death notice of a classmate, and I stop in my tracks, remembering some incident that was our connecting point. Fun-loving Johnny, the class clown, who took me to a party in the tenth grade. He died so young and at his own hand—and although I can barely remember his face, I feel such desolation at the thought of him.

Another layer. Layer upon layer of never-ending grief!

My precious friend Marcia lost her husband, Tim, to brain cancer, and right after his death the lock on the front door broke. She called someone to fix it, and it wasn't fixed correctly. "I could have handled it at any other time," Marcia said, "but to me that broken lock was a symbol of the loss of the protection that being married had given me. I went crazy."

Little did she know it wasn't over. Layer after layer, grief accumulates, like the peel of an onion.

After Tim passed away, Marcia battled two kinds of cancer, tolerating months of intensive treatments. Her best friend moved away, and she left her church, feeling emotionally deserted and misunderstood. All of this brought up the pain of her childhood and the feelings of abandonment she'd experienced at the hands of an angry, abusive father.

Still, she somehow managed to get by. Barely.

Then Marcia's much-loved cat died and that was the final—absolutely "more than I can take," throw-in-the-towel, what-else-can-happen—proverbial straw.

How many layers of grief can a person possibly endure?

The loss of a beloved animal can very well be the straw that breaks the camel's back. You've managed to handle the "big ones." You've managed admirably, but the day your pet dies, you come apart! You lose it completely. I've seen it happen time and again, and it's happened to me.

My cat Ya made my life more bearable during my year of chemotherapy. I would be so very sick, and Ya would curl into the curve of my body for hours at a time. He stuck with me through it all, and for a while after treatment was over, he'd often meet us at the door, lead us to the bedroom, leap on the bed and look at us expectantly, as if to say, "Come on, let's be sick some more!"

One day Ya didn't come when we called. We searched the woods—he never went far. Every day after that, we hoped as we came up the drive. Finally I knew he was gone forever, and I wrote this eulogy:

Dear Ya,

I guess you are really gone. This morning a fluff of your yellow-orange fur skitted across the driveway; but when I reached for it, a gust of wind swept it up to the sky. That's when I knew you wouldn't be coming back.

I can't help but remember the day we got you. You were just a ball of yellow fluff in Uncle Jon's hand. Dana and Mindy named you *Yata*, which is the Greek word for cat, because Grandma had been to Greece and learned that word. She told us how she laughed when she heard the Greek ladies call *"Yata, yata!"* and saw their cats come running. We thought that was funny, too.

You grew big and beautiful, and although you "frowned" a lot, we knew you loved your family and enjoyed the woods on "your" property. On occasion, we even caught you smelling the flowers.

I miss you and hope your last moments were peaceful. I would have liked to comfort you as you comforted me so many times. When I was so sick from chemotherapy, a greater companion than you could not have been found.

There's probably not a cat heaven; but if there is, I suppose you've met up with Goodie (Baddie is probably in that other place), Smokey the Pirate Don Derk of Don Day and my beloved Agamemnon. Perhaps you're all comparing notes on little girls you've known.

Grief accumulates!

As we pass from season to season through life, we experience the good, the bad and sometimes the worst!

I once was assured—by a well-meaning individual during a bad time in my life—that God was refining me, to which I answered, possibly with a rather indignant huff: "I'm refined! I'm refined!"

Perhaps it's true that God is refining us during our darkest, most desolate moments. Even when we don't want to be refined!

Which brings me back to my childhood in West Virginia, where there wasn't a lot to do in the way of entertainment. When we had out-of-town guests, the great attraction was Blenko Glass, located in the tiny town of Milton, an hour's drive west of Charleston. You've heard of Nowhere, USA? That's Milton, then and now!

Having arrived in town, you practically have to be a detective to find the road (it's been called The Dirt Road to Nowhere) that leads to Blenko. Look closely, and you can see it may have been paved at one time, perhaps right after the Great Depression.

The story of the Blenko family is fascinating in that founder William H. Blenko Jr.'s childhood intrigue with furnaces birthed in him a lifelong passion for decorative glass. William came to America from London in the mid-1890s to produce hand-blown glass for stained-glass windows.

After several attempts, many failures and bankruptcies, and at least one return to England, William decided to give it one last try. He was 67 years old when he moved to Milton, West Virginia, choosing that tiny town (to this day called "Milton on the Mud") for no other reason than its plentiful supply of natural gas and access to the railroad.

Instead of bringing in outsiders, Mr. Blenko taught the residents of Milton and the surrounding area his glass-blowing techniques. The rest is history. Today, Richard, a fourth-generation Blenko, is at the helm of this world-renowned company.

The aesthetics of the place haven't changed much over the years. Even after you've parked your car in the dirt lot, you keep wondering if you're there. Chances are you've missed the tiny sign, and it's hard to believe the huddle of shack-like buildings, each just a cut above an old barnyard lean-to, could be the source of the stunning art glass that is displayed in *la-de-da* galleries worldwide.

When I was a child, I loved the visitors' tour, which still consists of nothing more than moving at your own pace along a wooden walkway—a sort of indoor-outdoor arrangement that allows you to follow the glass-making process from searing blob of sand to finished *objet d'art*. There are exquisite vases of all shapes, sizes and colors, as well as pitchers, compotes, candy dishes, platters and fruit bowls.

I could have hung over those rails forever, the heat of the ovens burning my face like the Caribbean sun. I was mesmerized as those magnificent artisans (humbly disguised as workmen in singed, stained and tattered overalls) danced the dance of the refining process to the deafening music of the glowing ovens. As though a spell had been cast over me, I'd inch my way along on tippy-toes, not missing a single motion—from blob on the end of a long pipe, to fiery oven, to the master craftsman who with great skill—and with such force that his cheeks looked like they might explode—blew shape into the nothingness. With long wooden paddle in hand, a second workman (dance partner, if you will) would dart in, out and around the fiery mass with such precision that at times the men and the glass seemed like one finely tuned apparatus. Shaping! Turning! Spinning! Trimming! Fluting! In and out of that hellish furnace. Burning. Searing. Making beautiful!

I learned early on that no two pieces of hand-blown glass are alike. Each has its own unique identity. Often an anomaly will become the very thing that sets a particular piece apart and gives it value. I devoured the pamphlets and books that told how the different colors are created, becoming especially intrigued with how the rare ruby-red glass is made.

The story goes that for centuries, since Egyptian times, artisans had tried to perfect this highly valued red glass. Other hues were created fairly easily when substances like magnesium or cobalt were added. Not the elusive ruby red!

Eventually, after years of being obsessed with this mystery, William Blenko Jr. uncovered the secret. It wasn't some chemical, not some special dye or paint. It was sensitivity to heat! The secret was in the heating process itself. At that moment of discovery, Mr. Blenko is said to have proclaimed, "Eureka. I have found it!"

When Wayne and I married, our Blenko glass wedding gifts were proudly displayed on our Danish modern coffee table in our tiny apartment in Whiting, Indiana—and later in our first house in Wheaton, Illinois. Living in the Chicago area, we learned it was fashionable to visit the Chicago Art Museum. Fashionable *and* an inexpensive way to spend a Saturday afternoon! (We're still members, but the price of admission now includes plane tickets from Nashville, dinner and a hotel room!)

From our first visit to the museum, we were drawn to the magnificence of the art glass. In the mid 1970s, when a Tiffany exhibit was unveiled, we were enthralled and found ourselves going back time after time. We met Louis Comfort Tiffany (we didn't really *meet* him, you understand; he's dead—what I'm

saying is, we were introduced to his work), a glass artist of genius proportion. And to think his family was famous for their
dealings in silver and fine jewels!

Can't you just hear the insouciant young Louie saying to
his father, "Nah, I'm not really interested in diamonds or emer-
alds or amethysts or rubies. If you don't mind, I think I'll just
chip up some glass and make lamp shades!" Can you imagine
his father's response?

Of course, Louis Tiffany was so much more than a designer of intricate mosaic lamps; he was the most eclectic of artists.
He was a master of vases, enamels, ceramics—and jewelry! He
was a painter, an interior architect, a decorator and a designer!
And the most celebrated of his creations were his stained-glass
windows. Louis's approach to them was so very sensory, and he
drew inspiration from what he saw in nature—insects, birds,
landscapes and flowers.

Falling in love with the Tiffany windows (I never cared
much for the lampshades) eventually led me to discover that
some of the world's most glorious stained-glass windows were
created in Milton on the Mud! In fact, Blenko windows grace
such renowned structures as Rockefeller Center, St. Patrick's
Cathedral, St. John the Divine, Liverpool Cathedral and the
Washington Cathedral.

These discoveries led me to another designer of stained-
glass windows, Marc Chagall, and a whole other perspective—of
funk and flamboyance! (Wait! Is this another trip to the alligator farm on the way to the family reunion? I think it is!)

I can't possibly visit the Chicago Art Museum without making my way past the Tang Dynasty Buddha-like sculptures (who,
if the placard is true, will guide us to salvation), through the hall
of arms and armor, past the priceless silk vests embellished with
jewels and worn by bishops and priests in the eighth century, to
sit on the bench before the magnificent Chagall window. You

could stay there all day and still not soak it all in. Chagall claimed to prefer a life of surprises (me, too!), and his work shows it.

On my last trip to Chicago, I went straight from the soothing angels hovering in the windows of Second Presbyterian Church to the topsy-turvy floating figures from the imagination of Marc Chagall at the Art Institute. Then I made my way to the gift shop, where I was surprised to discover Blenko glass displayed right smack between Tiffany and Chagall! I felt as though I'd come full circle. (With a stop at the alligator farm thrown in free of charge, of course.)

As I've traveled the country and heard the life stories of men and women who've been through the fire, it doesn't escape me that it's the heat—the fire—that has made them who they are today. No doubt about it! They've danced the dance of the refining process to the deafening music of the glowing ovens, and the Master Artisan has been faithfully doing His work. Shaping! Turning! Spinning! Trimming! Fluting! In and out of the hellish furnace. Burning! Searing!

The Master Artisan's touch has been upon my friends: Lois, Peggy, Ed and Jan, Nancy and David, Candy and Dave, and Marcia. And on many others I haven't mentioned, like Susan and Chuck, Dana and Barry's dear friends, who so lovingly care for their severely disabled, best-dressed-girl-in-town, Natalie. And Bill Cooper (Wayne's college roommate) and his wife, Ginny, whose son-in-law murdered their daughter and grandchildren and set fire to the house to cover his crime. And on *you*, my precious reader and friend. His touch has been upon you who have faced conflagration of great magnitude. Cancer and heart disease, Alzheimer's, loneliness and despair. Broken locks. And broken hearts.

But these friends of mine are not clothed as were the Greek ladies in the black drapes of mourning. These are vibrant people of great beauty and celebration. Each one a work of art—a Sotheby's, Christie's, Buckingham Palace, *Musee du Louvre*-quality *objet d'art*!

To quote Mr. Blenko, "Eureka. I've found it!"
It *is* the heat!

Unleashing Your Inner BHL!

To truly be the people God intends us to be, we must have empathy for others. And I'm not talking about sending a card and taking a macaroni casserole, dear reader!

Empathy means identifying with another person to the extent that you vicariously experience her feelings and emotions. It's going beyond the obvious and getting involved in the other person's life. It's offering your shoulder to lean on while you wipe away the tears.

Think about someone you know who needs you. Needs you to listen. Needs you to be there. If you can't think of anyone, call your church. Or if you don't have a church, call the church on the corner. Volunteer to stand in the gap for an individual or family that needs help.

A Lame, Lousy Limerick

If you're down—too discouraged to pray,
Put this book down and go right away
To the Scripture and probe
And read about Job,
Who had more than his share of *Oy vey!*

A Pithy, Provocative Quote

When her grief is beyond words, hush! No words are needed.
Just be there.

ME (IS IT OKAY TO QUOTE YOURSELF?)

Note

1. Nancy has written wonderful, helpful books for people who are dealing with grief. I hope you'll visit her website at www.nancyguthrie.com.

CHAPTER 9

Some People Spell It with an "F." I Prefer a "PH."

Unleashing Your Laugh

Whew! I think it's time to laugh. Laughing is good exercise. It's like jogging on the inside!

But maybe before you can unleash your laugh, you'll have to find it. Whether it's been lost, repressed, *repossessed* or run over by a Mack truck, I hope this book will inspire you to laugh loud—and often! Not at me, not at my stories, but at life.

What happened to that hair-trigger funny bone you once had? Remember how you used to laugh in junior high school? Think for a minute. Remember the first time you saw a picture of the opposite sex *naked*? You don't remember—yeah, right! Do I have to remind you? It was in health class, and you couldn't wait to get with your friends and giggle your guts out. *That's* the kind of laughter I'm talking about.

For whatever reason, as we get older we seem to find fewer and fewer reasons to laugh. I'm not talking about the half-hearted titter you make when your husband tells a dumb joke, or the sound that sneaks out when one of your children does something cute but slightly embarrassing, or even the thing you might *think* of as a laugh but which looks to those around you more like a grimace. (You know—that look you have at a wedding reception when everyone but you is doing the chicken dance!)

The laughter I'm talking about rekindling is the kind that causes your face to take on the characteristics of a Shar-Pei puppy and your eyes to spurt tears like a leaky water hydrant. The laughter I'm talking about causes you to hold your stomach and rock back and forth—maybe run for the bathroom! The kind that shakes your insides and then shoots out like fireworks to every part of your body so you feel it from the tips of your pink-lacquered toes to the top of your big hair!

Do you guffaw at the obvious? The *embarrassing*? Or do you pretend it never happened? Like the time you were introduced before an audience and your slip fell all the way to the floor. (It happened to me.) Or the day you were at an important business meeting and your fabulous new jacket fell open to reveal a black-lace-covered boob? (Me again! And by the way, what if you didn't cringe at that b-word? And though you'd walk on your lips before you'd say it yourself, what if you didn't judge those of us who think there's nothing wrong with it?)

Wait! I think I'm on to something—and so early in the book! When my fingers typed the word "judge," it dawned on me: *That's* the problem. Why didn't I think of this before? It's profound!

We judge each other. I do it and so do you, and we show it in our actions. We cringe! We tsk-tsk! We shake our heads sadly in dismay.

Then there's that certain look—the one that radiates disapproval in neon lights. It happens when that self-righteous feeling comes over us, and in our minds we're saying:

"I'd never act like that."

"I wouldn't go to a church that does things that way. Crazy Pentecostals (or Methodists or whatever) . . . mutants, all of 'em!"

"My children are smarter than yours."

"I'd never let myself get that fat."

"I'd never wear jeans that tight—let alone be seen in public with that big hairdo!"

And on and on, we go.

I say, "Yes, you would! Yes, you would! *Yes, you would!* So would I." (Especially if I had the butt for wearing tight jeans.)

Why are you so prissy? I ask you. *And why am I so self-righteous?* Why do we take ourselves so seriously? Why can't we tolerate each other's quirks and foibles and learn to overlook the nonessential differences that divide us? Why do we get "all het up" (one of my dear, departed Aunt Annie's favorite expressions) about things that don't matter anyway? Just think! We could be enjoying each other! We could be laughing ourselves silly together!

I often speak to cancer survivors, having written the book *I'm Alive and the Doctor's Dead: Surviving Cancer with Your Sense of Humor and Your Sexuality Intact,* so I pay attention to the "home remedies" people come up with. I can't tell you how many folks believe that laughter has cured them. Some have bought every funny DVD and audio tape they can lay their hands on and have spent days on end immersed in comedy. I heard from one man who swears the funeral home had been called to pick up his remains when he decided to try the humor cure. Sure enough, he revived and laughed himself well. (Okay, I'm exaggerating—get used to it.)

It's a proven fact (don't make me stop and prove all my facts, girlfriend. Life is short: I don't do windows and I don't do research!) that besides making us healthier, laughter makes us forget our problems. It gives us peace of mind and causes our spirits to soar. We become more popular because everyone wants to be around us. And . . . *ahem!* . . . our sex lives improve. (I definitely didn't research the cause-and-effect factor in that last bit of info, but talk amongst yourselves—do your own investigation!)

Warning! Skip the next story if you tend to be self-righteous, hypocritical or think your bodily emissions smell like rose petals. On the other hand, read it! Perhaps you've waited all your life to admit to something so obvious . . . and laugh about it! What I'm talking about, to put it bluntly, is *that* body noise I myself have only come to acknowledge in recent years.

Like you don't do it, ha, ha, ha, *ha!* Give me a break!

Please don't think me disrespectful when I say this. *But,* my dear, departed mother is rolling over in her grave—*spinning* perhaps!—over this particular subject matter. She was such a lady! We her offspring were taught to be proper at all times. And acknowledging *that* body noise would not have been proper under any circumstance.

Imagine how beside myself I was when in college . . . on choir tour . . . on a bus (which meant there was no place to run), I tickled one of the tenors in the tummy and, to my horror, the tickling unloosed a toot loud enough to tear through the transonic barrier. (Note the brilliant use of alliteration. This is why I'm a writer.)

Okay, okay! No more alliterations. And no more of those dratted parentheses the editors like to slap my wrists over. What I'm trying to convey is that "*that* body noise" is such an obvious thing—a hilariously funny thing!—and what do we do? *Pretend it doesn't happen.*

When I married Wayne, I discovered he didn't have any problem acknowledging it at all and furthermore saw great humor in it. I blamed it on the fact that he was from farm country and that those plow jockeys from Indiana have seen and heard it all. (His boss, a fine churchgoing Christian, even said the *sh*-word, as in "Get out to the barn and shovel out the—" It's not a swear word, you know, but let's just call it "manure" for the tsk-tskers in the audience.)

I'm sorry to say that my husband's brand of humor will be mired forever in the barnyards of the Midwest—a junior high school mentality if ever you saw one. He'll laugh at anything and everything. Fortunately we hang with friends who don't have to have an excuse to laugh, either.

I've told you about our Sunday night fellowship group. I've told you we're like a family and that we all love to eat, and most of us love to cook. We follow—painstakingly, mind you, we are really quite devout—the biblical exhortation that says wherever two or three are gathered, someone brings baked beans and another brings banana pudding.

I hate to say this right out loud, but it's true: God is not our one and only focus. Food runs a close second. And sometimes, if the truth be known, it's the other way around. But I digress.

One night, Tad was called on to close the evening with prayer. Tad is an enthusiastic, caring oncologist; an enthusiastic husband to Rosemary; an enthusiastic father to Lacy; *and* an enthusiastic pray-er! We bowed our heads, and Tad began his enthusiastic prayer. It went something like this:

> Dear God, you are a loving God . . . blah, blah, blah. We are unworthy . . . blah, blah, blah. We often fail to meet Your expectations . . . blah, blah, blah. *So God, please forgive us our falling shorts.*

It took a second or two for us to realize what he'd said. Lynn got it first and sputtered. Then Evelyn sputtered. I laughed out loud, and Jimmy guffawed. Wayne howled! Soon everyone was pounding each other and belly laughing.

I'd like to think God was laughing, too. Perhaps going home with merry hearts did us more good than finishing the prayer.

Maybe God knew exactly what He was doing when He permitted me to have cancer. Perhaps He knew it would be the best thing that ever happened to me. It's true! In many ways my life is better. Family and friends are more precious, every day is sweeter, and I'm not nearly so worried about the age-old question: *What will people think?* And that lets me do and say things—and *laugh* at things—I might have passed judgment on before.

The year I was supposed to die, the year I was on chemo, was a tough one. And it's a strange dichotomy, but while I was experiencing every side effect known to man, I was also savoring the moments, appreciating life more than ever before. I remember once driving down the expressway and catching sight of a double rainbow. I couldn't pull over fast enough! It took my breath away. I got out of my car and soaked in the beauty of it, as though it was my last moment on Earth.

And I was laughing as I hadn't in years!

That Christmas we had our usual party for friends and family, and since this would be my last (at least that's what we thought), Wayne and I worked harder than ever to make it a memorable event. A few days before Christmas, Wayne came home with a rubber ice mold in the shape of a frog and proudly announced that he was going to make a green frog for the punch bowl.

When our guests were all assembled for the party, and may I just say it was quite a dramatic moment in the history of our family, Wayne sashayed (my husband is quite large, so his sashay in itself is quite a sight) out of the kitchen, punch bowl held high; and with a decided flourish, he placed it on its faux gold pedestal in the middle of the magnolia-and-holly-laden table.

"Ta-da!" he effused. Guests sucked in their breath. Eyes popped.

"Oh *my*," they responded, clutching their breasts. (Did I just say what I think I just said? Did I add drama where drama did not exist? Well, just *go* with it. Humor me!)

It wasn't long before the Annual Green Frog of Christmas (as it's now fondly referred to, despite the fact that it only happened that once) began melting—and as it melted, it made a noise.

You guessed it. *That* noise! That Green Frog of Christmas blew the bottom bassoon. Tooted the trouser trumpet! Let sound the colonic calliope! Over . . . and over . . . and over again.

For the person standing nearest the frog, it was anathema—and let me tell you, gentle reader, perception is everything. Everyone knows a frog made of ice does *not* expel gas.

Or does it?

Soon all the party guests were clustered at the other end of the living room, as far from the punch bowl as possible, with "it wasn't me" looks on their faces. It was a rather short evening, as I recall.

What I remember most is that after the prim and proper guests bid their *adieus*, the raucous few of us remaining laughed our guts out! It felt good and it felt right. It felt just like junior high school.

So here are some questions to ponder: Why did it take a crisis of life-and-death proportions to bring out this unabashed joy and laughter?

And why don't we laugh like that all the time?

Unleashing Your Inner BHL!

What tickles your fancy? Reruns of *I Love Lucy*? On a sad night of our lives, when we'd been hit by some devastating news, our daughter and her husband, Dana and Barry, and Wayne and I chose to watch the movie *RV* starring Robin Williams. Believe me, it lifted our spirits—if only for a while.

Do you have a particular friend who likes to laugh? Invite her over for coffee.

Or try reading a Martha Bolton book. Martha was a writer for Bob Hope, Phyllis Diller, Wayne Newton, Mark Lowry, and others, and her books are easy to find and full of funny stories.

A Lame, Lousy Limerick

Let all your inhibitions depart!
Wipe the frown off your face, for a start.
Then loosen that buckle,
Let out a loud chuckle!
And have a good laugh when you—oops, no . . .
Have a good laugh from the heart!

A Pithy, Provocative Quote

*You don't stop laughing because you grow old. You
grow old because you stop laughing.*
Michael Pritchard

CHAPTER 10

Gold Lamé Is the New Black, and Big Hair Has a Spiritual Purpose

Unleashing Yourself to Simple Christianity

Can I assume that since you picked up a book with God's name in the title, you aren't a total atheist? And you won't be offended if I approach the subject of God?

Are you sure?

Now that we've bonded (we have, haven't we?), I don't want to step on your cute little toes and cause a massive un-bonding!

I can't claim any deep knowledge of theology myself, except what I've picked up in the parking lot at church. But here's what I'm thinkin'.

I'm thinkin' maybe we've complicated the whole God thing.

For years I believed that if I had a better brain and could study more, read more books, take another class and understand more sermons at a deeper level, then I would have arrived. Where? I'm not sure. The Pearly Gates maybe?

The truth is, I'll never read all those books, never take that class, never study as I should and never understand every word of every sermon. And okay, okay! I know what you're thinking: I'll never have a better brain! I didn't and don't and couldn't and probably won't, if that makes any sense. But if you do and can and could and will, then more power to you.

Meanwhile, I'll just have to settle for simple!

A vast wealth of knowledge about God doesn't mean a whit if you don't understand the simple stuff. And think about it: You can be eruditely brilliant in systematic theology, hermeneutics and biblical exegesis—and just plain miss the excitement of it all!

When it comes to the labels that define us as Christians, I understand the basic differences among Protestants, Catholics, Presbyterians, Methodists, Baptists and the what-have-yous. I've been a few of them in my lifetime. The thing I'm having trouble with these days is the people who keep popping up on TV, lumping us all together, claiming to represent us and saying really dumb things.

I'm talking about those pear-shaped evangelists and pudgy, multi-chinned preachers—and women whose hair looks as though it might have been wound around an oatmeal box, the color of which surely must have come from some other planet!

I once attended a convention of religious media types, and there were people with hair up to Jesus—and that was just the men! It's a good thing there weren't any ceiling fans, or surely some poor soul would have suffered a broken neck. I can just picture it: someone being caught up in the twinkling of an eye—not to meet Him in the air, but to be wound like a top into the whirling dervish of the blades, then twirling in midair till the medics arrived.

Having said all that, I must admit: I'm not consistent. (Have you read thus far and not figured it out, dear reader?) As has been established, I do sorta kinda like big hair (as long as it's not a Disney color), and I recently read that big hair is coming back, which will be a huge boost for this book! I didn't even know it went away!

To my way of thinking, big hair makes a statement. Think about it before you banish your teasing comb to the garage sale. First and foremost, it adds height, and almost everybody looks better with a little height. It adds drama. It even makes your legs look longer. (I made that up, but it *is* my book.) And when combined with oversized earrings, fishnet stockings and strappy stiletto heels, well, you are practically announced before you enter the room.

Please don't think me gaudy, my dear, tasteful, always-do-the-right-thing reader, but in addition to sporting rather big hair, I often wear a feather boa when I speak. Just as almost everyone looks better with fluffed-up hair, a feather boa adds some ethereal, mystical aura that can't be accomplished with a dickie.

Note: I say "almost everyone looks better." An exception might be a nun! I once threw a feather boa around a nun's neck— at one of my speaking engagements, at the podium, in front of all her associates—and God help us! All I can say is, if looks could kill, I'd be six feet under with my stone-cold hands folded across the bodice of my best lace dress.

Why it didn't dawn on me she was a nun, I'll never know. It was a Catholic hospital—and although she wasn't wearing one of those big flowing thingies on her head, had I looked in the direction of her shoes, I could have figured it out. (My Catholic neighbor Joe, after reading a draft of this chapter, decided it's okay for a nun to wear a feather boa as long as she doesn't get into the habit. *Boo! Hiss!)*

What were we talking about? Oh, yes! How we don't want to be identified with those weird people who've appointed themselves as spokespersons for all Christian people—sometimes even on primetime TV, for heaven's sake!

Questions persist: Am I part of the Moral Majority? Well, I'm not part of the immoral majority. Hmm. If I join the Moral Majority, can we take a vote and kick some people out?

Am I for family values? Of course I'm for family values! I clip those coupons from the paper every Sunday. Just last week we got half off at the dry cleaner's and a free Arby's beef and cheddar sandwich.

Am I conservative? Liberal? That depends on what we're talking about. Catsup? Hairspray? What?

Am I an Evangelical? It has a nice ring to it, unless it means that if I don't tell people about God, it won't get done. I happen to think God is sovereign and doesn't need me for anything. Not to write books, not to speak, not even to play an accordion and pass out pamphlets on street corners. He can accomplish His will just fine without me, thank you very much. Do I want to be part of it? You betcha!

As long as I'm getting a few things off my technologically enhanced bosom, here's another thing that makes me crazy: those TV preachers who make demands of God. Sometimes the demands are accompanied by a crescendo of organ music and a blow to the head that makes the afflicted person fall flat on the floor. I'm wondering if (at least until the show goes off the air) the resulting headache is so severe that it's worse than whatever the person was suffering from to begin with.

Do I believe God can do anything and everything, including zapping folks with His Spirit? I do, although I've never experienced it. But let me just say, I know show business when I see show business. What is God thinking about all this craziness, I ask? Maybe He has a viewpoint.

My friend Bob Benson (now in heaven) once was channel surfing and came upon a TV preacher ranting and raving like a madman. Bob was transfixed.

"I lost my voice awhile back," shouted the preacher, "and the doctor said I'd have to be quiet for a year. I'd have to stop preaching and rest my voice."

The reverend then related the rather one-sided conversation he'd had with God.

"God, I want you to heal me right now," he said. "I know it's Your will, God. You need me! You need me to preach on TV—to tell people about You and warn folks about hell!" By this time the preacher was practically shrieking and shaking his fist toward heaven.

"Losing my voice could not be Your will, Lord. So heal me. Heal me right now!"

Zap! He was healed. On the spot! Never had another problem speaking from that day on.

My friend Bob, a country-boy philosopher, said, "I think maybe God's side of the conversation went something like this: 'Oh, Brother Jones? Just hear Me out. Your losing your voice was part of My plan. I had such a good year ahead for you and Me. I pictured our being quiet together without distractions. I had things I wanted to talk to you about, things to teach you. But Brother Jones, it's easier to heal you than listen to you go on about it. So, zap!'"

Might I, when something bad happens to one of my family members, request a zap? Might I make demands and promises to God that I can't possibly keep—perhaps even try to bargain with Him? Might I lie down on the floor and kick and scream at the very Ruler of the universe?

Yeah. I probably will. I'm human. And, as you've figured out, inconsistency defines me.

But let me ask. Are *you* always and forever consistent? Didn't think so.

The fact that God often uses more conventional methods rather than a zap is more to my way of thinking—and I'm surmising that more often than not we don't have a clue how it works.

I'm 23 years out from having had cancer. Do I know exactly why I got well—or how? Nope. In the big picture I think God used a lot of things to bring about my healing: the love and care of my family, the prayers of those around me, the genius of my doctor, the harsh regimen of chemotherapy, the laughter that became so important to my spirit, and undoubtedly the awareness of His Spirit that permeated my being as I began to recognize Him anew—in the loving faces that surrounded me and in His handiwork, the glorious world that encompassed me.

If "Thy will be done" can be trusted, then doesn't it stand to reason that God wants what's best for us? Somehow I understood that as a tiny little girl—before I was confronted with legalism. I knew that God was in control and that if you loved Him with all your heart, life would pretty much work out. Growing up and getting too smart for my britches made me think I was as smart as God, and I only gave Him a call when I was desperate.

In the church I grew up in, I was bombarded by manmade rules and opinions, and it often left me befuddled and confused. Don't get me wrong: I treasure the church that was the foundation of my faith. Never do I forget that my heritage is in those sweet, plain faces who loved every mischievous bone in my little body. And oh, dear God in heaven! It's where I learned the Scripture that propels every moment of my life.

Let's face it. Like it or not, it's all part of my story, every bit as much as having my tonsils out or falling down the steps at that birthday party and having to have stitches. It's what's made me who I am today.

I guess you could say I've come full circle to believe as I did when I was a child, that God is in control and if I listen to His voice, life will work out. To His honor and glory, not mine, I might add.

It propels me to "dance" the Christian life, rather than try to figure out the theology of it. And when I dance, I smile. When I dance, I sometimes laugh out loud! As to big hair, fancy jewelry and feather boas, let me just say, "I couldn't possibly serve God without all the trappings." And did you know? Gold lamé is the new black!

Now it's time for a story.

You've heard me talk of my childhood persona, Mrs. Vandertweezers. A few years ago, I brought her to the page—I wrote a children's story about her that pretty much describes that blissful time in life before I knew there were rules. While

I've had several successful children's books, this one is yet to be published. I have no great urgency to get it to the masses. It's very personal. The little girl in the story is me.

Every morning Mrs. Vandertweezers got dressed as though it was the most important day of her life— because it was!

She put on her mother's discarded silk blouse and rolled up the sleeves. She arranged her favorite jewelry around her neck: a purple choker with matching bracelet and earrings and a pendant with a gigantic—almost real—diamond.

Her very fashionable high-heeled shoes let her plain ole toes poke out of the holes. Her mother said, "No ma'am! You may not paint your toenails today, tomorrow or the next day." And that was that!

After all, she'd learned a Bible verse that said, in no uncertain terms, that obeying your parents is right. She intended to do right.

"Decisions, decisions," said Mrs. Vandertweezers as she chose a hat from her vast assortment. "Hmm. Today I'll wear the one with the wide, wide brim and the long peacock feather and the veil down to there." (The hat had been a special gift from her church school teacher, "Miss Stevey," who wore a different hat almost every single Sunday of the world.)

The final touch was an animal around her neck that bit its own tail. It once belonged to her Aunt Ginny, who gift-wrapped it, tied it with a big bow and wrote "To: Mrs. Vandertweezers" on the attached card.

"This is the day the Lord has made," Mrs. Vandertweezers said as she turned this way and that in front of the long mirror. She twirled merrily.

"Let us rejoice and be glad . . . and be glad . . . and be glad in it," she sang.

It was her verse of the week. "Don't forget to use it in everyday life," Miss Stevey said every week before dismissing class. "See you next week!"

Smokey the Pirate Don Derk of Don Day rubbed against Mrs. Vandertweezer's legs. "Time to go for a walk, sweet baby," she said, picking up her cat, dressing him in doll clothes, and laying him on his back in the doll buggy.

"Don't forget to stay within eyesight, Mrs. Vandertweezers," said her mother. "I'll just go out and pull a few weeds."

Off they went up the street.

Next door, Miss Eubanks, a retired teacher, was relaxing on her big porch with a cup of coffee.

"Oh, Mrs. Vandertweezers, how are you this morning?" asked the neighbor. "And how's the baby?" Her smile almost covered her pretty brown face.

"This is the day the Lord has made," said Mrs. Vandertweezers.

Miss Eubanks smiled an even bigger smile. "You are so right. So very right!"

The next house was a duplex. The Jenkins family was friendly in a strange sort of way, but they never failed to walk all the way to the curb to greet Mrs. Vandertweezers heartily.

"Lookin' good, Tweezers," they said, getting her name wrong for the millionth time. "And such an unusual baby."

They scratched Smokey the Pirate Don Derk of Don Day's ears, and poked each other in the ribs and rolled their eyes.

This is the day the Lord has made. Let us rejoice and be glad in it, thought Mrs. Vandertweezers, although she didn't say it out loud and wasn't exactly sure why not. Nevertheless, she smiled a big, neighborly smile.

"I'd be happy to watch your toddler someday while you do your chores," she said. "Call me anytime. I'm quite trustworthy."

The family in the next unit was very unfriendly. They always gave Mrs. Vandertweezers funny looks. And they didn't speak. Ever! They sniffed and stuck their noses up at her sweet baby.

"This is the day the Lord has made. Let us be a grouch and not be one bit glad in it," Mrs. Vandertweezers whispered under her breath, but she smiled her big, neighborly smile and picked up the trash the garbage man had dropped and put it in her pocket. She couldn't wait to disappear behind the big hedge, high as her head.

"Let us rejoice and be glad in it," the nuns at the convent said cheerfully in response to Mrs. V's "This is the day the Lord has made!" greeting.

Often Mrs.Vandertweezers was invited into the convent for ice cream. If asked, Sister Barbara would play a little tune on the piano, and Smokey the Pirate Don Derk of Don Day was allowed a small dollop of ice cream. (Sometimes Mrs.Vandertweezers thought about being a nun, but she couldn't possibly give up her fancy clothes and her sweet baby cat, not to mention the fact that she wasn't even Catholic.)

The children in the schoolyard waved to Mrs. Vandertweezers. "Hey V! Like your shoes. Like your hat. What's the cat's name again?"

"Me-OW," they said right in Smokey the Pirate Don Derk of Don Day's face, which to Mrs. Vandertweezers seemed a very impolite thing to do.

"Me-OW! Me-OW!" Smokey turned his ears back in a cat-like frown.

"Let us rejoice and be glad," Mrs.Vandertweezers said, as she approached Jolly's grocery store.

"Hello there, Mrs. Vander-whatever," said Mr. Jolly in his jolly voice.

"Oh, that cat!" he said, changing to his not-so-jolly voice and giving poor Smokey the most unjolly-like scowl imaginable.

"This is the day the Lord has made. Let us rejoice except when there is a cat around," Mrs. Vandertweezers muttered. But she smiled her big, neighborly smile and offered to finish sweeping the walk.

"I'm very good at sweeping walks," she said.

At the corner, which was the absolute limit of where she was allowed to go, she turned around and headed for home.

All the way home she repeated the words of her Scripture verse. Past the grocery store, past the school, past the convent, past the very unfriendly people whose names she didn't know, past the Jenkins family and past Miss Eubanks.

Mr. Jolly gave her a thumbs-up; the children meowed; the nuns waved; the unfriendly people gave her funny looks and made sniffing sounds; the Jenkinses poked each other in the ribs and rolled their eyes; and Miss Eubanks smiled.

"This is the daay thaaat the Looord haaas maaade. Let us be glaaaaad and reeee-joiiiice in it!" Mrs. Vandertweezers sang one last time at the top of her voice, as she turned into her very own yard. "Some people get it and some people don't."

The end.

What could be more simple? Living out your life, trying to connect with others, and doing what's right, even when folks laugh or try to block your good intentions. Some people will "get it" and others won't. But that's God's problem. And it shouldn't change your thinking as long as you're doing right.

I'll soon be working on a Mrs. Vandertweezers Postmodern Bible Translation (the *MVPBT*)—complete with study guide and concordance! Watch for it!

Unleashing Your Inner BHL!

Think simple. For instance, think about the Twenty-Third Psalm:

> He makes me.
> He leads me.
> He restores my soul!
> He is with me.
> His rod and staff comfort me.
> He prepares a table . . . He anoints my head.

It's about Him, dummy! It's not about me. And it's daily. And it's *so* very simple. Duh! Even I get it!

A Lame, Lousy Limerick

My writings are often profuse
But you can see that I'm often confused
Am I this? Am I that?
Do I know where I'm at?
Inconsistencies? You'll just have to excuse.

A Pithy, Provocative Quote

*Live simply. Love generously. Care deeply. Speak
kindly. Leave the rest to God.*
Anonymous

CHAPTER 11

Somewhere Under All These Trappings, There Must Be a Church

Unleashed from the Unholy Trappings of Church Life

A while back my friend sent me a greeting card with the famous painting *American Gothic* on the front. Every time I see that picture of that shriveled-up, old, sourpuss of a couple, I wonder whose case of hemorrhoids was worse! Hers or his?

The man holds a pitchfork that might seem like an innocent garden tool were it not for the ominous look on his face—an expression that says "I'm gonna kill somebody before this day is over." The woman in question resembles Granny from the old *Beverly Hillbillies* show—on a bad day! You can practically see the hostility etched across her stern face.

The punch line inside the card reads: "Don't speak to them, Harold—they don't go to our church."

The card was from my friend Deb. It was a follow-up to a conversation we'd had earlier about how as children, each of us thought our own church was the only True Church, and that *we* were the only people who would go to heaven.

Even though Deb is half my age, was raised in New Jersey (I was raised in West Virginia) and attended a totally different denomination, our memories are very much the same. The two of us laughed that, had our observations been correct, there would be very few people in heaven—and most of those who managed to slip in would be grouchy old malcontents, much like the couple on the card.

Both our fathers were on various church boards, and we'd heard the discussions. We knew who always caused problems. We knew exactly who voted down the new water heater, the new organ, the new carpet, the new youth center. We knew who could be counted on to give dirty looks to "the youths" who wanted the youth center! Or heaven help us if we were invited to visit that church down the street that *had* a youth center. *They* weren't the True Church! Obviously, we were.

If I could live my life over again, I'd study religions. Not religion per se, but *religionS*. I'm not one bit curious about theology or doctrine, the tenets of the faith, the dogmas or the eschatological reasoning of it all. I just want to know what makes a person choose a certain church, and why five minutes after they join—their name barely dry on the membership roll—they think they're so dad-gum right!

I also wanna know why it's often the very church that should be nurturing us that keeps us from being that authentic Big-Haired Lady we long to be. Do you know how many poor souls have been chewed up, spit out and stomped on by people in the church?

Are crazy things done in God's name, or is it just my imagination?

For one thing, I'd like to know what would possess a person to go to a church that believes in snake handling, for goodness sake. Hey, I heard that gulp! You with my book in your hand. *You!*

Remember, I *am* from West Virginia and I know a thing or three about snake handling—a practice that still goes on there and in other Appalachian regions yet today.

Now that I've got your attention, let's take a little side trip to an alligator farm, shall we? No! Make that to a snake-handling church! But before we go, let me defend West Virginians, who always get a bum rap for being uncouth hillbillies. Most of us *do* wear shoes. Our tattoos *are* spelled correctly. Yes, collards under glass can be quite a delicacy. Some of us even have our very own Spam key (mine is engraved), thank you very much.

And—write this down so you'll remember—snake handling officially began in Tennessee, *not* West Virginia.

Not to drop names, but one of my childhood friends became the world authority on serpent handling. (I must stop here and ask, dear well-connected reader, can you claim to know someone of that stature? Wrack your brain. Didn't think so! I'm serious about stature. To this very day, whenever there's a mention of snake handling in the news, my friend is quoted as an expert.) Author and theologian Dr. Mary Lee Daugherty was (she died not long ago) a sophisticated, highly educated lady who held advanced degrees from such mugga-mugga institutions as Princeton and Georgetown. As a theology major, she became interested in religion as it relates to rural America. That pursuit eventually led her to a study of, yes, serpent handling! Hers was a pragmatic approach—she called the practice "a sacrament."

Mary Lee would traipse deep into those West Virginia and Kentucky hills and hollows, and she would emerge with colorful stories that would make your hair stand on end. Her firsthand account of a religious practice that you and I might call downright madness was spellbinding as she'd introduce you to the loud, intense music sung with guitars, accordions, tambourines and drums:

> They call us holy rollers,
> They call us serpent handlers.
> Well, holy, holy and tha's alright.
> Oh, if you're livin' holy, tha's alright.

Singing, dancing, speaking in tongues, a pulpit-pounding sermon and laying on of hands were part of every service. Eventually copperheads and rattlesnakes would come out of the boxes (along with a jar of strychnine or some other poison) and an unearthly aura—an electricity—would fill the air. Snakes were passed from person to person, twisting and slithering to the chant of "Jesus, Jesus, Jesus."

Of course, I say "hooey" to all that. One look at a venomous snake, and I say secure a burial plot, buy a shovel and start diggin' for Pete's sake! But then again, far be it from me to say that those sincere folks won't be in heaven. I hope they are! They would be interesting in a group setting. But I'm praying they'll leave their copperheads and rattlers behind on Earth.

When I was a little girl, I thought long and hard about which church I'd belong to if it were left up to me. Becoming Catholic was appealing, simply because the nuns who lived up the block were so kind to me and my cat. But when it came right down to it, I'd have taken the Episcopal church hands down! After attending one a few times with my friend Patsy, I knew I'd found home!

Ah, the magnificence of it all! The architecture. The stone façade. The imposing archways. The very opposite of our church!

They had magnificent stained-glass windows. We had no windows.

They had pews with velvet cushions. We had folding chairs.

They had a grand pipe organ that went all the way through the roof of the church, all the way up to God. We had an upright piano with a thingy attached to the keyboard that was supposed to make it sound like an organ (it didn't).

They had mahogany *everything*! We had cinder block everything.

I had no idea at the time what Episcopalians believed, but I knew that our creed could be boiled down to: "God said it, I believe it and that settles it for me." Our leaders boasted that

they had "discernment"—the implication being "we have it and
they don't." (Discernment. Could it be little more than a front
for being able to freely criticize those you don't agree with?)

The confusing issue for me was, just exactly what *did* God
say? I'd learned Scripture, but somehow it got lost in our
church leaders' interpretation.

I was sure God was mad most of the time. Sort of a "we
don't smoke, we don't chew and we don't go with boys who do,"
kind of thing—and smoking and chewing were just a few items
on an endless list of "we don'ts," which also included dancing,
cards, movies, theater, divorce and (would you believe?) women
wearing makeup!

They called it "barn paint." Even as a young child, though,
I knew a barn looked better painted. Now, as an adult, I do my
best to make up for the fact I couldn't (wasn't supposed to—
had to sneak around to do it) wear makeup then by freely
applying great gobs of it today.

Oh, how I longed to be an Episcopalian!

I was mumble-mumble years old with cancer and a not-so-
hopeful prognosis before I began to sort the myth from the
truth—cultural Christianity from orthodoxy. I could readily
embrace the fact that truth for all time is found in the ancient,
time-honored words of Scripture and that that's the very way
God reveals Himself to us.

What I rejected was some of the interpretation, which was
nothing more than opinion. It still goes on today. Sometimes
right there on "Jesus TV." Good grief!

Not long ago I was invited to speak to an Episcopal women's
conference. The leader said, "Our ladies are coming alive in Jesus,
and we feel we can trust you as a speaker. We feel you wouldn't
be a caricature of the Evangelical," which I took to mean that
I could be trusted to stay away from social issues. And since
God hasn't called me to speak on social issues (I'm more into

reveling in the way God brings us through crisis with our joy and sense of humor intact), I'm thinkin', *What's the big hoop-de-doo deal?*

As often happens when I speak at a church retreat, the ladies blessed me more than I blessed them. So hospitable. So giving! So many invitations for cocktails (which you don't get in a Baptist setting).

The next day was Sunday. Sitting in that small but magnificent church—one of the oldest in the nation—the beauty of the sanctuary, the reverence of the congregants, the liturgy with its heartfelt responses, the intentional walk forward to kneel and celebrate the Eucharist were like a balm to my peace-seeking soul.

After the service I walked the hallowed grounds of the graveyard that wrapped around the church. I visited the final resting place of bestselling author Eugenia Price—also a West Virginia native and friend of the family—who dug deep into that Georgia soil to uncover, and in her own magical way, vividly preserve and enhance the stories of its memorable inhabitants.

This setting, like a page out of history, was a reminder to me that at times my soul craves liturgy . . . orthodoxy . . . history . . . and that to deny my spirit these reviving moments is to deny God's blessing on my life.

Another speaking event made its imprint on my spirit even more—and in the most wonderful and unexpected way. After agreeing (in writing) to speak at a women's conference in Ohio, I discovered they intended to close the afternoon with a foot-washing ceremony.

And I freaked!

Where could I turn with my questions? Like what do you do about your pantyhose? In my mind's eye I could see a church full of people—everyone's shoes thrown off and scattered about, socks hanging from the chandeliers—and someone (the pastor, maybe?) moving from person to person with a bucket of soapy water, doing the smelly deed as the water got murkier and murkier. Ugh! The stench!

I tried to think of ways to cancel. Then I remembered that the woman who'd invited me was a perfectly sane, dignified, mover-shaker type of business woman, and she would never, ever put me in an embarrassing situation.

Yeah, right!

I tried to think of it as one more of life's adventures, and as the day drew near, I found out that a dear friend who lived in the city where the conference would be held was planning to attend. I hadn't seen her in years. I was excited. It did occur to me, however, that I should warn her to leave early if she didn't want her feet washed. On the other hand, if she chose to stay, at least I'd have a comrade in what I was no longer calling "an adventure." By now it had come to be known as The Ordeal.

It turned out to be one of the sweetest, most memorable moments of my life. An event that makes me cry whenever I speak of it. I'm weeping even now as I write.

The women—old, young and in-between—took their time tugging their chairs into a big circle in the fellowship hall; and as they did, they stopped to chat with each other—to laugh and giggle and hug—with an intimacy that was foreign to me, at least in church.

"Sister," they called each other. "Sit by me, Sister McCollum. Let me help with your chair."

"Oh, Sister Swart, remember? You were the first ever to wash my feet. I was no more than 10 years old."

"I remember, child. And your grandmother was the first to wash mine."

The leader, with a lovely porcelain bowl full of clean, warm water and a delicate linen towel draped over her shoulder, began the ceremony. She knelt in front of a young mother and began to lovingly caress her feet with water. Then she slowly dried them with her towel. And as she did, she expressed words of gratitude and kindness, affirming the young woman as a mother, a friend and a fellow church member. She acknowledged the "bad year" she'd had and praised her that she'd managed, with God's strength, to make it through admirably and with grace. She pronounced a blessing of encouragement for her future.

Affirmation!

It seemed to be the mantra, and it occurred to me how desperately we need to be affirmed. To be noticed. To have someone recognize our progress. To be empowered with the courage to go on.

We chatted each time the porcelain bowl was washed and replenished with warm water. We seemed to have all the time in the world as I watched in awe. The crisp, white linen towels were plentiful, as were Kleenex for the tears. One after another, the women washed each other's feet (with or without pantyhose, in case you were wondering).

As the afternoon progressed, I felt like an observer. But I longed to be a participant. I wanted to be "one of them"—to know the camaraderie of this time-honored ceremony. Then, as though she'd read my mind, Barbara, my childhood friend, was kneeling on the floor in front of me. With tears glistening on her cheeks, she proceeded to wash my feet with such dignity you'd have thought she'd practiced for this moment all her life.

"This is the greatest privilege of my life," she said for all to hear. "Our mothers were dear friends, and I think in a way, they washed each other's feet. They loved each other and took care of each other."

At that moment, in my mind's eye and as vivid as could be, I saw her mother, Bertha Ashley—a starched bib apron tied around her ample middle—announcing in a loud voice that left no room for argument, that she'd be "taking over the kitchen." This was only hours after my daddy had died.

As Barbara gently dried my feet, she looked into my eyes and expressed how proud she was of me, assured me that my mama would be "so proud of me" if she were there, and suggested that perhaps our mothers were, in fact, smiling down at us from above. Finally, she said a blessing over my future.

Now when I think of foot washing, I no longer think, *Ugh!*

Instead, I think of that soul-shaping experience in Ohio. It taught me that to be a true friend, we must take on the role of "the lesser one." The servant. We must be willing to wash one another's feet, even if only figuratively, with our words—words of affirmation and encouragement—and our actions.

Somewhere along the line I've figured out that God is available to all who believe, through Jesus, His Son—in whatever space they call church or not in church at all—and that He can sort out our earthly attempts to explain Him and celebrate Him.

So here's my question. And it's a goodie.

If Jesus walked this earth today, where would He go to church? Think about that one!

My friend Nan Gurley, actress, playwright, comedienne, writer, wife, mother and someone much to be admired in every way, has not only asked that question, she's also taken it one step further and written a song about it. Nan performs it with a Christian comedy group called the Glory Bugles. (Check out www.glorybugles.com. You won't believe it!)

As I drive along the city streets I am confused to find
That everywhere I look there is a church of every kind
Now this presents a problem that makes my heart to lurch
If Jesus walked this earth today where would He go to
   church?

Would He sing *a capella* or play an instrument or two?
Would He stand up and raise His hands or stay down
   in His pew?

Would the Lord be sprinkled or would He be immersed?
He'd have to do it our way or else He'd be accursed.

Chorus:
If Jesus walked this earth today where would He go to
    church?
He'd need our firm direction or find Himself
    besmirched
This question has an answer that the righteous all can see
He'd find the one true fellowship and go to church
    with me.

He couldn't find one on His own, He'd have to meet my
    friends
He'd need a fancy preacher to help Him make amends
Or else He'd stumble into the wrong theology
He might not find religion without some help from me.

Ye generation of vipers, I'm tired of warning you
If there is only one true church, there isn't room for two
They say we're in the Bible Belt, but I think that you
    should see
You may be up a notch or two but the buckle is with me.

Bridge:
And when He comes back to this earth
I have just one wish:
He'll find His bride on Wednesday night
with a covered dish.[1]

Here's a thought. Maybe if the farmer and his wife from
the painting had done a little foot washing, they'd have had a

better marriage, a better life and (one can only hope) a better family picture!

And maybe a good foot washing would have led to other things, if you know what I mean, and there'd have been a few young 'uns in the picture.

Unleashing Your Inner BHL!

Ponder this prayer. Pray it if you dare!

Dear Lord,

Give us friends from all faiths, and let us gain strength from them.

Thank You for our loved ones who are Episcopalian and Catholic, for the stirring pageantry of their worship (which I experience most fully on Christmas Eve). They give us permission to express our need for liturgy and quiet, introspective worship.

Thank You for our "died in the wool" Baptist friends, who never let us forget the truth of redemption—that there is one way to heaven through Jesus Christ, our Savior.

Thank You for the spiritual vibrancy of our Pentecostal friends and allow us to experience at times their joyous abandon.

Thank You for Your sovereignty and the covenant You made to Your Body, so beautifully understood by the Presbyterians and others of Your reformed churches.

Thank You for those who are Methodist. They remind us of our responsibilities to carry out Christlike social justice in the world around us.

Thank You for the Mennonites, dear Lord, who teach us about simplicity and nonviolence.

Thank You for our Nazarene friends, who teach us to embrace holiness.

*And as to the churches of the African-American tradition,
let us learn to be one and together fulfill a determination to see
Christ's gospel fleshed out in unity that knows no boundaries.*

*Accept our thanksgiving for the diversity that marks the
life of His Church; but remind us evermore that there is one
Body, one Spirit, one Lord, one faith, one baptism.*

Amen.

*P.S. And as for our differences? Oh, please, God. You be the
one to sort that all out!*

A Lame, Lousy Limerick

At washing feet I was a rank amateur
Thought it was something I couldn't possibly endure
Said, "My feet are alright,
I washed them last night
Plus I'm long overdue for a pedicure."

A Pithy, Provocative Quote

*I always prefer to believe the best of everybody—
it saves so much time.*

RUDYARD KIPLING

Note

1. Nan Gurley, *If Jesus Walked this Earth Today, Where Would He Go to Church?*, copyright © 1985, Big Leg Music. Used by permission.

CHAPTER 12

Love Your Outfit! Does It Only Come in Large Sizes?

Unleashing Yourself from Rude and Negative People

Ever noticed that people with dogs get away with much more than people with cats?

I haven't finished the research, but I think the reason is that dogs never hold you accountable. They never question you. In fact, I hate to say it, but they mostly act like fools! They always give you that adoring look that says, "Oh, my goodness, you perfect person, you! I've never seen you make a wrong decision in your life. You're absolutely *right* about everything. Let me just lick your face!"

Dogs will listen as you talk to your friends, their faces shining as though they're part of the conversation, so enraptured by you that they inadvertently drip drool all over your best Tony Lama boots. "Oh, my mistress! How very wise you are! I *never* would have thought of that in a million years. Tell me more—snort, sniff, sniff, snort!"

A cat owner, on the other hand, has to watch everything she says, everything she does. Cats listen in on your conversations too (while pretending to sleep), but don't be fooled. Just when you're at your wittiest, prettiest, wisest and best, the atmosphere will change. Your feline friend will come alert, lay his ears back, look at you, and then turn his attention to the blank wall. And he'll say (you *feel* it, rather than hear it), "You're *not* all that!"

A cat will make you question each and every word that comes out of your mouth—make you question your very *existence*, for goodness sake! Yes, your beloved cat can ruin the whole day.

When, on occasion, you speak authoritatively on a subject you've researched from the ground up (at the National Archives, mind you), your cat will look you square in the face, give you that hooded-eyelid stare and say, "I'm not so sure about that, Einstein. Maybe you'd better check your facts. Rethink it and get back to me."

Dear reader (and dog owner that you may be), by now you surely know that I'm pulling your touchy, defensive (albeit shapely and lovely) leg. Yes, I happen to be a cat owner, but I do love dogs. And we'd have one (my husband's heart cries out for a boxer) if only we could stay in town long enough to feed and walk it.

My cat loves me dearly, but he cares not a whit who puts Fancy Feast on his china plate and water in his crystal bowl. As far as he's concerned, I was placed here on Earth to open cans. And he much prefers to walk himself, thank you very much—from the warmth of the sundeck door, to the cozy daybed in my office, to his command post at the top of the stairs, to the overstuffed chair in our bedroom and back again, with naps wherever and whenever the mood strikes.

Oh, if it were only animals I had to deal with—I could handle that! But people are the problem. I could be such a good, upstanding citizen and a fine Christian woman if it weren't for other people.

Is it my imagination, or are there those who, for whatever reason, seem to have no accountability in life? They just say and do pretty much whatever they dad-gum-well please without regard for anyone else's feelings. And as far as body language goes? Think cat!

The question is, How do we get unleashed from these negative people who intimidate us so easily so that we can *be* the
life-of-the-party, cute, witty, delightful darlings we were meant
to be? How do we live in Big-Hair-Lady style without having
our very *guts* sucked out of us by all the naysayers and the toxic
aura that surrounds them?

Is revenge an option? (Don't say this hasn't crossed your
pious mind, dear friend.) Like maybe baking your best from-
scratch cake and replacing the sugar with horseradish and red
pepper flakes, then leaving the cake on the offender's doorstep,
ringing the doorbell and hiding in the bushes to see the reaction?

Oh, shush your *tsk-tsking*. You know you'd do it in a heartbeat if you thought you could get away with it!

How about letting the air out of their tires while they're in
church? And yes! Many of these types *do* go to church and are
the very ones who'll report you to God if and when you don't.

Even though I'm basically a kind and wonderful person, I
admit to having a backlog of nasty comebacks, just in case the
opportunity to use them ever arises. Catty remarks like: "Oh! I
see that the shag carpet in your dog house matches the shag
carpet in your living room. How clever!"

Or "I noticed you have cobwebs. Did you know you could
throw a handful of glitter on them and make them sparkle?"

Or how about this one: "Nice perfume. Did you marinate
in it?"

If you choose to be more direct, you could go with: "Don't
upset me. I'm running out of places to hide the bodies."

For the record—and I'm sure you already know this, being
the figure-it-out kind of person you are—a comment from one
person can be rude, while the exact same thing coming from
someone else (say, a close friend) can be fall-on-the-floor funny.
I'm just waiting for a chance to use the one about the cobwebs
on Peggy when she tells me for the umpteenth time she hasn't

dusted! Truth be told, she never dusts. Once a year she just calls the cops and reports a robbery. They dust for fingerprints, and she's good to go for another year.

It's Peggy who's responsible for the title of this chapter. She's a tiny little size two and a merciless tease. Sometimes when I'm strutting around in a new outfit, she'll say in her cutest lil' voice: "Ooooh, I just *love* your outfit. Does it only come in big sizes?"

Everybody falls out laughing, and I'm not offended in the least. Peggy loves me and I love her.

On the other hand, Joy and I were once enjoying ourselves in a little shop in Florida, when a snooty salesclerk announced, "Sorry, ladies, we only carry small sizes. Our clothes don't come in large!" (We were a size 10 and a size 12, so go figure.) We practically crawled out on our bellies. But that was then! Now I'd have a comeback. I'd say . . . well, never mind! You don't wanna know!

Even though I have this backlog of great comebacks stored up, I always try to do and say the right thing—overcome evil with good and all that. It's not because of *my* goodness. It's because of my mother. (You gotta wonder whenever you meet up with one of those rude, hateful people: Does she even *have* a mother? And does she think that Bible verse reads "Do unto others *before* they do it unto you?")

My mother never let me off the hook. She'd say, "First of all, examine your own heart and be sure you aren't part of the problem; then try to turn a bad situation around." She said that people are usually mean-spirited because they have issues we don't know about. She said we should be kind so that the person in question can pass that kindness on to the next person, and so on. Mother could have written, produced and directed the movie *Pay It Forward*. I'm sure she came up with the concept.

Anyway, one late night I was doing my email when an IM popped up.

"You stupid deceiving person, you!" it said, to my absolute shock. "You despicable woman . . . blah, blah, blah!" (Some of the blahs are unrepeatable.) "You take advantage of cancer patients. You'll pay for this! I reported you for credit card fraud."

I answered with one word: "What?"

Here's the story: This bile-spewing woman had ordered my book *I'm Alive and the Doctor's Dead* from my website. She'd requested that it be sent to her very sick sister in California, and though the credit card charge had gone through, her sister had not received the book.

The woman said she'd sent me two letters I'd not responded to, and said she knew in her heart I never intended to mail the book.

I happened to find her two letters in my spam folder, and they too were vile! "You deserve to have people know what a disgusting, cheating, unethical person you truly are [swear word, swear word]. Watch out, lady! You [blanked] the wrong person."

Yikes!

What's a person to do?

I'm sure you're one step ahead of me here, dear reader. You're reading my mind! Yes, my first thought was that she was a wretched old bat—a miserable, disgruntled malcontent who made a habit of taking out her wrath on others. And yes, I could barely contain myself! I was ready to tear loose and shoot back a response that would make a sailor blush.

But then . . .

Then something magical happened. A gentle breeze wafted through my open window and lifted my gossamer drapes of silk into a wild, whirling-dervish of a gypsy dance. A billowy cloud of fairy dust whooshed in—up and around, kissing everything in its path. And the fairy dust caught the moonlight and twinkled like stars seen through the eyes of lovers. And . . . and . . . the rapturous tones of a (what's that thing called?) a . . . a xylophone, that's it! The rapturous tones of a xylophone filled the air, and I clearly (don't doubt me here) felt the brush of angel wings.

And then *Fabio* emerged through the mist and caressed my cheek . . .

Har har. Just kidding!

So here's what really happened: I heard my mother give a big sigh. No words, just a sigh! "Please, Mother," I begged, "it would be so much easier to give this woman what she deserves. Please let me tell her off."

Mother won! (All the way up in heaven—and she won!)

Perhaps this woman's life is out of control, I channeled. *Maybe she loves her sister desperately and lives in mortal fear that she'll lose her. Added to that, there could be a dozen other reasons that might cause such bad behavior—health issues of her own, perhaps (mental instability?)—and not getting your book wasn't even the real problem. You may never know.*

"Okay, Mama!" I replied. "Maybe you're right. I should give her the benefit of the doubt—and turn this situation around."

And so, I groveled!

I wrote a letter of apology, saying how sorry I was and that I honestly couldn't imagine what had happened to the book since I had the shipping receipt right in front of me. (I did have to at least point that out, to save a little face.) I assured her that her money would be returned and that I had $100 worth of books (including the book lost in transit) and gifts ready to send to her nice sister. (By this time I'd begun calling them the Nasty Sister and the Nice Sister, clear evidence of the conflict in my spirit!)

"Again, I apologize," I wrote. "I *do* try to give my life to encouraging cancer patients and would never take advantage of anyone. As I signed the books, I prayed for your sister—who, by the way, you could take lessons from, you rotten-to-the-core, mean person, you!" (No! I didn't say it, but I sure-as-shootin' thought it! And no, I didn't *really* "channel" my mother either.)

In a few days, I got an email from the Nasty Sister. She thanked me profusely and then asked, "You prayed? Oh, you are a Christian? I had no idea."

Duh, I thought.

"My sister isn't," she said. "Her heart is hard and she may be dying, and she's shut her mind to God. She won't listen to anything I have to say!"

Double duh, I said to myself.

And . . . *and* . . . *AND!!!!!* You'll never believe what she said next. You'd better sit down for this one.

She asked me to please pray for her sister, that she would turn to God!

"In a pig's eye!" I said, right out loud.

And yeah, I know what you're thinking. But before you judge me too harshly, let me say, I did pray. I prayed for *both* sisters—in four religions and seven languages, for heaven's sake!

Then I did a terrible thing. I sent an email to my friends, telling them the story with a little questionnaire:

Shall I:

a. Pray for the sick, nice sister and begrudgingly forgive the nasty sister—and pray for her, too?
b. Offer my stem cells to the sick, nice sister and send anthrax to the nasty one?
c. Enhance the story and put it in my next book?

I got responses from everybody, but the best came from my gun-slinging, target-practicing friend Mike. It said: "You wan' I shud do her in? Invite her to da gun range wit' me? Huh?" (said in my best gravelly Brooklyn-mobster voice).

What a good idea, I'm thinkin'. Then I remembered I don't want Nancy Grace all over my "case," and I'm not anxious to be a feature story on Court TV.

Dealing with people who pull you down and suck the life out of you is a fact of life. Once in a while, though not very often, you can just rid yourself of a person who causes you angst and distress. I've seen it done. And how do I admit this? I was once on the receiving end of such a tactic.

I was gotten rid of. *Perfect me!* Can you imagine? And I hadn't even been mean.

When our children were young, Wayne and I had dear friends we loved to get together with, though they lived in a different city. We thought nothing of the six hours that separated us and would drive back and forth as often as possible. We'd eat and talk for hours, stay up late playing games with our kids, and we'd feel genuinely sad when the weekend was over. We couldn't get enough of each other, although I guess you could say they *did* get enough of us! Well, not "us." It was *me* specifically.

One day out of the blue, Liz (not really her name) said, "We don't want to be friends with you anymore." My mouth must have dropped open to my knees. She was one of my best friends. I was nonplussed. I had no words! I couldn't even manage to ask why. Fortunately I didn't have to.

"You have a negative effect on me. I don't know how to say it, but you wear me out!" she said, followed by a long, pregnant pause. I still couldn't utter a response.

"It's not just when I'm with you that you wear me out," she said. "You wear me out even when I'm not with you. You wear me out when I *think* of you."

We changed the subject and finished the weekend as cordially as possible. And home they went (can you believe they were at *our* house?), never to be heard from again. It seemed a huge loss to our family but we moved on, always wondering how they were and whether they missed us.

Years later, I had just finished speaking at a women's conference, and up walked Liz, as if nothing had happened and just long enough for us to exchange *you-look-great-how-are-you-doing-how-are-the-children-blah-blah-blah* pleasantries.

End of story.

So, here's my question. Which are you? And which am I? Positive and encouraging? Or might you and I be part of the problem? Do we pull others down? Do we even *know*? Have we ever stopped to assess any damage we may have caused? *Eeek!* Apparently I hadn't.

What about our body language? Do we give off negative, nonproductive vibes? Are we *en*couragers rather than *dis*couragers? Will we go out of our way to turn evil into good? The answer to those questions just may be the final word on whether we're true Big-Haired Ladies or not!

Dogs got a bad rap at the beginning of this chapter with all that sniffing and snorting and dripping and drooling. But think about it: Perhaps they're the true heroes, those cute, delightful, authentic little bigger-the-hair-the-closer-to-God bundles of fur, bones and guts. Maybe they're the real encouragers after all.

But don't tell my cat I said that!

Not that he'd care.

Unleashing Your Inner BHL!

Well.

I suppose at this point my best suggestion would be for us to staple our lips together so we won't be tempted to use all those nasty barbs we have stored up, ready to use at the drop of a hat. Not that there aren't people who deserve them, mind you. I'm just saying, this is one way we could do our part for the betterment of humankind. Maybe once in a while we could even turn the situation around, do a return-evil-with-kindness kind of thing.

What if you're the negative one? Have you thought about that? What if you're the person who's holding the bucket of ice water, ready (and willing) to douse any idea or plan, or to squelch another person's spirit? And what about your body language?

If you're that person, somewhere deep down in your mean little guts is a cute, darlin', witty, intelligent, passionate, authentic, interesting, life-of-the-party, POSITIVE person.

For heaven's sake, *let her out!*

A Lame, Lousy Limerick

Sometimes I really get mad
(But dear God, is it really that bad?)
If I wouldn't get caught
I'd be nasty a lot
And getting even would make me feel glad.

A Pithy, Provocative Quote

A bumble bee is considerably faster than a John Deere tractor. Don't corner something that you know is meaner than you.

AN OLD FARMER'S ADVICE

CHAPTER 13

I Heard God's Voice, and He Said to Go Get a Massage

Unleashing Yourself for a Day of "Shear Madness"!

Being the astute reader you are, I'm sure you've caught on to the obvious—that being the Big-Haired Lady doesn't in actuality mean the dimensions of the hairdo. *Right?* It's an attitude. A bigger-than-life attitude.

Having the BHL attitude, though, certainly doesn't take away from the fact that we should look our best. I would be remiss not to mention the importance of the BHL presentation package—"the outward appearance," so to speak.

Even people in Bible times were into image—and a beauty regimen. Read the book of Esther in the Old Testament. Before a young girl could go into the presence of King Xerxes, she had to complete 12 months of beauty treatments, and we're not just talkin' hair and makeup. There were massages galore! At least that's my interpretation. It explicitly says, "six months with oil of myrrh and six with perfumes and cosmetics" (Esther 2:12). What else could it mean, unless they were drinking it? (Please feel free to write me with your own interpretation.)

The end result—the breathtaking beauty of those women—must have been even better than those makeovers on TV. It says the king delegated eunuchs to oversee these stunning virgins. I surely don't have to tell you what a eunuch is, do I? Or why it is they could be trusted?

Today, beauty is a bazillion-dollar business, much of it coming from my very own bank account—and girlfriend, a good citizen always thinks of how she can boost the economy, so go out and find yourself a good salon. *It's your duty!*

There's a beauty business on every corner. I checked the Yellow Pages to see how many were listed right here in Nashville (a lot!) and did a quick evaluation.

Abracadabra. I'd recommend that salon in a New York minute! I can't tell you how often I *need* a little abracadabra! Make that *a lot* of abracadabra!

All Eyes on You. Affirmative again! That one appeals to my ego. Can't you picture yourself coming down a magnificent stairway in a fabulous dress like Barbara Streisand in *Hello Dolly*? Time would stand still! And, yes, all eyes *would* be on you, my lovely enchantress.

Acts of Faith. Not a good name for a beauty salon. Think about it! I'd stay away from that one.

Alchemy Salon and Curious Gifts. What is alchemy, and what, pray tell, is a "curious gift"? I say if you have to look it up in the dictionary, it's a firm *No.*

Eye Candy. Yes, for obvious reasons.

Starlene's. No!

Billie Jo and Helen's. No! Though the gossip could be excellent.

Conception. Are you thinking what I'm thinking? No! A thousand times no!

Brazen. Yes. And I can't even tell you why.

As to *Above and Beyond,* just the name of it makes me think these people will knock themselves out for you: "Oh, dah-ling, put your feet up, let me get you a magazine and a bottle of Evian. Let me put little cotton balls behind your ears."

Unless . . . unless . . . *Above and Beyond* has a spiritual meaning. Get it? Above and beyond? Like, say, judgment day arrived
and God snatched you up. You'd be *ready*. You'd look good.
You'd make a great first impression! (Well, hopefully it's not a
first impression. If that's the case, you're in big trouble.)

Another possibility—and why for goodness sakes, didn't I
think of it before, having originated the BHL lifestyle and all—
Above and Beyond means the *height* and *width* of the hairdo! This
could be your best bet of all!

Hold on. I'm thinking as I go. Has anyone considered nam-
ing a line of beauty products "The Bigger the Hair the Closer to
God?" Well they will now that I've thought of it.

Yet another idea is emerging. *Yes, yes!* How about a church
named The First Church of the Bigger the Hair the Closer
to God? I *love* it! There would be on-site hairdressers on
Sunday morning, the choir robes could double as shampoo
capes and . . .

Oh, never mind—I got carried away. I don't see that one
becoming a reality anytime soon.

One of the most uproariously funny stage plays of all time
is *Shear Madness*. It's what they call a long-running show, which
means it's usually performed in smaller theaters, perhaps off
the beaten path, and it keeps going, I suppose, until people quit
coming. The website says it's been seen by over six million people around the world. At least two dozen of those people are
folks we've taken.

It's a wacky murder mystery that takes place in a unisex
hair salon. Above the shop lives the landlady, Isabel Czerny,
who is murdered—and everyone in the cast has a reason to have
done her in.

The set is wildly tacky and so are the characters. They
include, among others, a mouthy, gum-popping, overprocessed
blonde. And (call it like it is) an equally overprocessed gay guy.

During the intermission the audience gets involved in the action by questioning the actors as they mix and mingle with the crowd. Then, during the second act, the crime is solved based on input from the audience—and the culprit is rarely the same character two nights running.

Perhaps the reason the play is so popular and folks come back time after time is that even if you've seen it before, you never know how it will end.

Another reason could be that we relate to the setting. We've all "been there." We've frequented those beauty shops (or barber shops or nail salons) all our lives, where the characters are bigger than life, where "attitudes" abound, where gossip is rampant and where, in your heart of hearts, you know the conditions are ripe for a good old-fashioned murder mystery.

Like at my salon, when someone would inadvertently sit down under old Miss Mathis's favorite hair dryer. She passed away awhile back, but no one can forget the murderous look that came into her eyes and the hateful way she gripped the handles of her walker when she saw someone under *her* hair dryer.

Unlike the newfangled shops where boys and girls prance around in black T-shirts to match their tattoos, sprayed-on jeans with Elvis belt-buckles and their hair moussed every which way, my beauty shop is a pretty ordinary place.

My daughter, before she moved away, used to go to a funky postmodern place, to a hairdresser who pronounced his name "Gar-doun" (Gordon, ya think?). Gardoun would run his fingers through Dana's locks and declare for all to hear: "Thees! Thees ees not hair! I make eeet hair! Ze freenge (fringe? bangs?) needs a treeem!"

One day Dana's curiosity got the better of her. "Gardoun," she inquired, "where were you born? Where do you come from?"

"Tull-a-*ho*-mah," he answered, in the same manner in which he might have said, "Pah-*ree*!" Tullahoma is a small country town a hundred miles east of Nashville. Apparently it's a little more hoity-toity than most people realize.

I, as you well know from the dedication page, go to Hair Villa to have my locks cut and colored and made *big*.

I'm sure you are picturing in your mind's eye a *villa* as in "a large and imposing estate in the country," as the dictionary would have you believe. Ha-ha-ha, I'm falling off my chair! A leee-tle misleading! Would you believe a modest brick structure down on Charlotte Avenue—beyond the Wal-Mart, beyond the doggy hotel, beyond the lodge hall—between the Cozy Cottage Antiques place and the gas station—with the neon sign in the window that says "OPEN" or "CLOSED" as the case may be?

Inside it's not too villa-ish either, but it's oh, so warm and friendly and is decorated lavishly for every holiday of the year. It makes me feel special. Like I'm worth the effort.

At Christmastime they serve fancy desserts and punch. The punch is just plain old everyday punch. Everybody knows you can't serve boozed up punch in a beauty shop.

Or can you?

I know a person . . . someone . . . a person very close to me . . . really close . . . okay, it was me . . . who got sappy drunk once on beauty shop punch. Don't go postal on me here, dear reader who is perfect and who never misses a chance to frown and make the tsk-tsking sound. Get a grip. Stop your cater-wauling! It's a sin-filled world and sometimes it sneaks up on you. And—as you might expect—I have an explanation!

One day, some years ago, in the days when we lived near Chicago, I got up early and took Wayne to work. We only had one car, and Thursday was my day to use it. That particular Thursday, I had an early appointment for a cut and color.

The beauty salon was beautifully decorated with holly and velvet ribbons; carols filled the air; the cookies and pastries were plentiful; and there was a big punch bowl filled with a frothy beverage that, at the time, I did not know would warm the cockles of one's heart. It was yummy delicious, and I warmed the cockles of my heart to the tune of five cups (maybe eight) in a row as I sat under a hot hair dryer.

When I stood up, I felt dizzy with Christmas cheer—a room-spinning kind of joy, actually—and I sang "Dancing Queen" using a hairbrush for a microphone. Then I sprayed everybody with the hose from the shampoo bowl and danced on the coffee table to "O Little Town of Bethlehem," which was playing on the sound system. Then I called my husband.

"Hey, honey! Hey you big ole handsome hunk of husband! How 'bout comin' down here and pickin' me up? I'll make it worth your while."

My husband curtly pointed out that he did not have the car—I did. When he questioned me further, speaking softly through gritted teeth (and letting me know he was not alone), I could tell he was not pleased. He worked for a very conservative, image-conscious organization (a Christian organization!) at the time. Had word gotten out about my (however innocent) indiscretions, it would have blown his career—and the organization's reputation—to smithereens and back.

Fortunately, he was able to borrow a car, pick me up and take me home, and by the time I got home I was back to normal. So we turned around and went back to get the car. (Following me here, dear reader? Again, think "full circle.") We had a good laugh, and he explained to me—and I don't know how he knew, coming from a Baptist home and all, but he did—that vodka can sneak up on you. It has no smell.

One more thing about hair salons and I'll change the subject. You'll never need a counselor, a psychologist or a psychiatrist if you have a good hairdresser. Trust me on that. And it's a fraction of the cost. A beauty shop is the best money you'll ever spend.

The second-best investment might be a massage. If you want the feel of a mini-vacation, save your pennies and make an appointment. The reason you must save for it (rather than put it on your Visa) is because saving makes you long for it—and the longer you long for it, the more precious it becomes, therefore making it more pleasurable when it happens.

Sometimes you luck out and a friend pays for it.

In fact, just last week I spoke in Indiana for my friend Gloria, and even though I'd been there for a few days already, she kept coaxing me to stay one more day. She said God wanted me to stay, which seemed at the time like nothing more than a conniving trick. I told her God needed me to get home and write this book.

"No," she said confidently, "God wants you to stay. I'll put it to the test. I'll ask Him to give us a sign. I'll call the spa, and if they have an opening tomorrow morning for the two of us to get massages, that will be the sign He wants you to stay."

Well, guess what? You'll never believe! The spa was, in fact, able to take us. And all I can say is, I'm humbled! I was totally mistaken about Gloria's being conniving. It was, without question, a case of divine intervention. Loud and clear!

Another friend of mine who believes massages and other spa treatments are a gift from God is Kay.

Kay called several years ago to invite me to speak at her women's retreat in Montana. I named my fee and asked a few questions, like what kind of group it was, how many times would I speak and for how long. Her answers were vague. I asked if it was a church group, and she said no. I asked what my topic should be and she said, "Whatever you want." I questioned why they got together, and again, I got no real definitive answer, except that they liked to have a good time. I asked where the women came from, and she said they were girls she'd picked up here and there, but that quite a few of them came from the Dayton, Ohio, area.

I finally concluded it was some weird cult—not that I was too good to show up to speak for a cult, mind you. I just didn't want to go alone.

"Can I bring a friend?" I asked, and she agreed that I could bring my friend Lynn.

Five years later, Lynn and I are still part of this crazy group (mostly Christian women, so it happens) called the Flamingos. Whenever we gather for our "retreats," our accommodations are luxurious, the catered food is out of this world, and the pool is Olympic size. The second day of the retreat is Spa Day, and 22 (count them!) beauty experts show up to give us massages, pedicures, manicures, facials and haircuts.

Kay loves the word "lavish." She believes that since God has been so generous with her, she should do likewise with others. She lavishes her friends—mostly young mothers who might not otherwise have such an opportunity—with ski trips and vacations, and caters to their every need.

Have you ever heard anything like it? Me neither! Every time I'm invited back to Kay's gatherings, I keep pinching myself to see if I'm dreaming or if life can really be *that* good.

Getting my hair and nails done on a regular basis is a *must* for me, and massages and pedicures are occasional decadent indulgences that boost my spirit. Some people have a hard time spending money on pampering, but I'm not one of them.

Perhaps your first thought would be to use that money to feed the homeless in Macadamia. God bless you. I wish I were more like you. I only ask one thing: Make sure you aren't all talk and no action. And that's all I have to say about that.

As for the gifts of my friends, I accept them freely—and I hope that my gratitude is as generous as their giving spirits. Don't be one of those people who can give but can't receive. "Oh, no! I can't possibly let you do that." "How can I repay you?" "Oh, no, I hate pedicures. Thanks anyway!"

I pray, dear reader, that someday your ship will come in. And when it does, dang it, recognize your ship when you see it coming! Know that it's arrived, and be ready to share it. Once you've enjoyed the good things, start lavishing them on others.

And for goodness sake, get yourself to the beauty shop so you'll look good for the pictures!

Unleashing Your Inner BHL!

If you want to be a Big-Haired Lady in body and spirit, treat yourself to an hour or two at a beauty salon for a cut and color—or a day at a spa. You'll be a new woman! Save for it. I promise you, it's worth it.

Better yet, keep on the lookout for a friend like Gloria, who believes God is in the "signs and wonders" business and sometimes gives a one-word answer: "Massage." Pray for a friend like Kay—or decide you'll be one yourself. Listen closely for the word "lavish."

A Lame, Lousy Limerick

Someday when you're having the blahs
Take the phone book and check out the spas.
Or get a hairdo at lunch
But don't drink the punch!
If you do you might break a few laws.

A Pithy, Provocative Quote

Never worry about numbers. Help one person at a time, and always start with the person nearest you.
MOTHER TERESA

CHAPTER 14

Old Is When You Hear Your Favorite Song on an Elevator

Unleashing the Wonderful, Wise Older Woman in You

This chapter has been the toughest one yet to write. You can't imagine!

Doing the research was nearly impossible. After searching the world over, I'm convinced there aren't many people who are willing to admit to the *O* word. (At least not *this O* word!)

What happened to those self-proclaimed old ladies I remember from childhood? Fluffy grandmothers with ample laps, comfy bosoms and time on their hands—not to mention a year's supply of safety pins hooked to their bra straps in case of emergency? Grammas whose lives revolved around afternoons of cuddles and coos with their grandchildren? Book reading? Storytelling?

Grandmothers today seem to be (as TV commercials would have us believe) romping the beaches of Florida, exchanging glances with svelte, too-good-to-be-true grandpas, neither of them worrying a whit about denture odor or bladder control. Safety pins on bra straps? How about *no* bra straps?

This isn't the first time I've given thought to the *O* word. Almost 10 years ago my friends Gloria, Joy and Peggy and I discussed it thoroughly. At the time the four of us were writing the book *Confessions of Friends Through Thick and Thin*, the subtitle of which turned out to be: "Now That We're Old Enough to Know Better!"

Make no mistake about it. We were not by any means admitting to being *old*. Heaven forbid! We were pointing out the fact that we've a vast wealth of experience, as in been there, done that; nosedived, crashed and burned; gave it to God, took it back; played tug-o'-war with God; lived, loved, learned, lucked out; picked ourselves up, brushed ourselves off and started all over again!

To sum it up: *Experience equals answers!* Duh!

Before we wrote our books, we'd learned a lot—felt we had a measure of credibility—and were ready to make ourselves available to help others muddle through the murky black moat, wrestle the hungry alligators, stagger through the thorny maze at the other side and fight the abominable giants lurking there. We would lead our dear readers to the great shiny castle in the sky. (And I have no earthly idea what all this means, but it sure sounds credible.)

In the introduction to *Confessions*, Gloria listed some things we'd learned:

> We now know that failure is not such a bad thing. It is life's greatest teacher.
>
> We know that we don't have to actually spend our lives doing what we majored in in college.
>
> We know that our real vocation is life. What we do at work just buys the groceries.
>
> It's okay if at fifty we still can't wait to see what we'll do when we grow up. In fact, we've wised up so much that none of us ever intends to grow up! We've known a few grown-ups and didn't really like them very much.[1]

This is the kind of wisdom, my friend, that can only come from having survived the moat, the alligators, the maze and the giants.

As our work progressed, we realized we needed an identifying word for our status that would not assault our senses. We rejected the obvious: "aging," "elder," "older," "advancing in years" . . . "old hag"!

And then we thought ourselves quite clever when we hit on something.

"Passages!"

Passages! Passages! Passages! We said it over and over, loving the way it rolled off our tongues. Someone pointed out that it made it sound as though we were still dynamically fluid—that not only were our brains in motion, but our bodies as well.

Like dancers!

Catching the excitement, we grabbed the concept and built on it. (We either build on each other's ideas or argue about them.)

"Subliminally, they'll picture us in tutus and ballet slippers," Joy said, as she pirouetted around the room. It was not the greatest moment in pirouette history, and I was pretty sure when it was my turn I couldn't improve on it. And furthermore, as I looked around the circle and pictured us—four slightly-past-their-prime ladies—in tutus, I couldn't help wondering if that was the image we were after.

The book has sold well and the four of us are still friends, but we never donned tutus for pictures or any other occasion. In retrospect, "passages" may not have been the best choice of words. "Passages" means "passing from one place, or from one condition, to the next." I can't help asking now, "From where to where?" and "From what to what?"

Is there a perfect age? And is a tutu a must-have in the larger scheme of things?

As to the perfect age, when I was 6, I wanted to be 10. A 10-year-old got to stay up late, cross the street by herself, wear whatever she wanted and have a friend over to spend the night.

When I was 10, I wanted to be 16. Oh, the life of a 16-year-old! Definitely the perfect time of life, if for no other reason than to drive a car. But somehow when I got there, being 16 wasn't quite *it* either—there were too many rules!

I was certain being old enough to go to college *was* all that and more. Now I can't remember a thing I learned there, other than that students could get in big trouble for climbing the water tower—and I only remember that because it goes on your permanent record. The going-to-classes part all runs together.

Surprise! Surprise! College wasn't *it*. All we talked about in the dorm was getting to the next stage of life—getting married. Oh, how we longed to wear that big white dress with the big satin butt-bow. That would really be *it*!

On and on it went, this search for *it*. You get married and that's good, but there's this nagging feeling that something is missing. Let me think! Oh, I know! It's kids! Everyone else is having children. Real fulfillment surely must come with having kids. Absolutely! Positively!

So you have a baby.

And after a year or so, you start thinkin' two children are better than one. In fact, three is a perfect number! Then one day you're trapped in traffic, trying to figure out how you'll get Molly across town for her dance lesson and Matthew the other direction to his soccer game. Frozen groceries are melting in the back seat because you didn't have time to stop by the house as you'd planned, because you were late getting the fifth-graders home from the field trip, because you had forgotten to pick up the permission slip, because you'd left it in your other purse, because the other purse didn't match the shoes you were wearing today.

You have an epiphany!

It will be when the kids are old enough to fend for themselves . . . no wait! *It* will be when they get through school, move out—*and duh!*—why didn't you think of it sooner?—the financial burdens will be *histoire!*

But then the kids are gone, fending for themselves (though not quite, because you're still sending checks), and you're working harder than you ever did. And with less energy!

And at last you realize: There just ain't no such thing as *it.*

"I'm getting nowhere," you say. "I might just as well just give up. Call it quits."

And then: "Eureka! That's it! Quit is *it!* What am I waiting for? Retirement baby, here I come!"

So you pack it up, have a garage sale, put the house on the market, buy a condo in Sunshine City and shop for white furniture.

"Yeah, doggy, this is it! Hey, Frank, is this *it* or what? Frank, are you listening to me? Frank! Wake up. Frank! Get your grubby feet off that white furniture!"

After a couple of months of *it,* you notice Frank is getting hard of hearing, or at best has developed "selective hearing" if you know what I mean—and I think you do. As for you, you've spent so much time in the hot tub, you remind yourself of one of those hard-as-a-rock, dried-up raisin masses that's been in the refrigerator way too long.

Not only do you stop looking at yourself in the mirror, but you begin to talk to yourself, asking yourself questions. If retirement's all it's cracked up to be, why does my back go out more than I do? And why do I plan my whole week around Enema Night?

What is *it*? What *is* the perfect time of life? I'm asking you, dear wise reader. I'm tired of coming up with all the answers!

Perhaps the answer is this: Grow old gradually and gracefully. (Although I must admit, because I'm an all-or-nothing kind of person, I've entertained the idea of doing just the opposite. Like, someday I'd just wake up and say, "I'll be old now.")

Seriously (or at least more seriously than before), old can be very appealing, depending on how you look at it. For one thing, choosing to get old means you don't have to worry about how you look. *Que sera, sera!* No more long hours at the beauty shop, dabbing at your oozing, smarting eyes while the color is applied.

"Hey, let it go gray, ole girl. Cut it off up to your eyebrows!"

And speaking of eyebrows, is waxing not the closest thing to torture you've ever experienced? And that's just the eyebrows and chin hairs . . . and maybe the mustache. As for the bikini line? Never mind!

Old means no more time sweating on the treadmill, unless, of course, you exercise for health reasons (I wouldn't know a thing about that)—as opposed to exercising in an effort to look like a siren.

And think about how good it would feel to release that demon named *What Shall I Wear?*

"Yessiree Bob, I realize I'm wearing four long-sleeved sweaters all at once. It's s'posed to turn cold. Besides, haven't you ever heard of—whoops, I must've dribbled there—layering?"

And think about this: No more pantyhose! You can wear those horrible old-lady knee-high things and roll them south to the ankles. Let go of the pain!

And speaking of pain, you can go braless. You can tuck your boobs into your waistband if they've drooped that far—and in case you think it's never been done, just ask my friend Peggy (not that she herself does it—like most of my friends in Nashville, she's had a lift) who claims to know a lady who *does* tuck her boobs in her waistband. (Forgive the run-on sentence . . . that one got away from me.)

The best reason for choosing to be old is that you don't have to think anymore. I ask you: In some strange way, is that not appealing? Just to let your mind go?

Have you ever noticed that some people start "talking old" long before they get there? It's like they're testing the waters.

"I just worry about that parakeet of mine—I'd hate to think she'd outlive me. Who will clean up her messes if I die?"

The other side of the coin is: Stay young! Make a commitment here and now to stay on your toes at all times. Euthanize the stupid bird and move on, for Pete's sake. Quit talking like you're 87 (even if you are) and stop saying whatever comes into your mind. Like how you don't sleep well anymore, when everybody knows you doze all day and your head practically rolls off your shoulders on Sunday mornings during the sermon!

When you really don't remember something, say in a firm voice: "Excuse me, but I have so much information in my brain computer that occasionally it takes me a moment to download. Did you know that in the last four years of the past century, we've been assimilating information at a rate of 50 times more per day—we're talking exponentially here—than we assimilated in the preceding 96 years?"

(No, precious one, I don't know if it's true. But if you say it boldly—with conviction and passion—it will become truth as you speak it. Exponentially? They don't know that word. They'll be impressed out of their gourd!)

Always have ready answers. "Well, I too am appalled at the political situation, and I intend to exercise my rights as a citizen. In fact, come next Monday, you'll find me in Washington lobbying on that very matter." (Again, relax! No one will ever check to see if you follow through.)

Another must is this: You have to be up on technology.

"Oh, let me Google that." Count on this as a stock answer for almost anything.

"A newspaper? You still read newspapers? I haven't dirtied my fingers with those for years. You know how black your hands get, not to mention what they'd do to my new white sofa."

(A reference to a new sofa implies you expect to live quite awhile longer.) "No, I get my news from the Internet! Have for ages."

When I weigh the pros and cons of getting old, I realize I'm not ready to make the switch. I have a standing appointment at Hair Villa and Silky Nails. My wardrobe is fairly fashionable—if a bit gaudy. I'm still reading and keeping up with current events, albeit via *People* magazine. I not only use email proficiently, but I have two—not one, but *two*—websites and add daily to my database.

There is that one thing, though, that still pulls me like a magnet toward the drip-and-drool side of the fence. Old people can behave pretty much as they please. I've already taken to sitting at the end of the pew on Sunday mornings and pinching men's backsides as they scoot by.

Occasionally someone will say, "Don't mind her—she's getting up there." Someone else will say, "But you'll have to admit, they must like it. Her row fills up in a hurry."

Unleashing Your Inner BHL!

This one's up to you, my friend. Your choice.

Don't age at all, age gracefully—or jump in with both orthopedic feet. But whatever you decide about growing old, remember this: Be your bigger-than-life, Big-Haired self!

Live each day as if it were your last! Live it to the fullest. If there's something that burns in your gut—something you want to accomplish—*do it now!*

A Lame, Lousy Limerick

What happened to the grandma who cooks?
Who has time to sit around and read books?
    She's gone off on a cruise

(Her perfume is perfuse)
And she's mostly concerned with her looks.

A Pithy, Provocative Quote

Age mellows some people, others it makes rotten.

HEARD IN ARKANSAS

Note

1. Peggy Benson, Sue Buchanan, Joy Mackenzie, Gloria Gaither (editor), Kathleen Bullock (illustrator), *Confessions of Four Friends Through Thick and Thin* (Grand Rapids, MI: Zondervan, 2001). You should also read our best-seller, *Friends Through Thick and Thin* (Grand Rapids, MI: Zondervan, 1999).

CHAPTER 15

What If We Find Out That the Hokey Pokey Really *Is* What It's All About?

Unleashed to Simplify

Life's gotten complicated. Don't you agree? Look around! We're meeting ourselves coming and going. Not only are we spinning our Michelins, but we're spinning plates on broomsticks like circus performers.

We're obsessed with trying to find better ways of doing things we don't even want to do, but we think if we ever *do* do what we don't want to do, we'll have made the task easier. (What did I just say? I'm not even sure myself!)

We sit spellbound in front of the TV, believing every over-the-top adjective that rolls off the silky tongues of those perfectly coiffed QVC hostesses. We just gotta have it! We breathlessly call in our orders and wait for the FedEx man. Surely our lives will be better, happier and more productive—and if not, with all those luxurious skin products, we'll look good trying!

Our hands sweat as we unpack the 27-step cosmetics regimen that looked so easy on TV, but which in truth will take 27 minutes longer to complete than the one we ordered last month.

The 300-piece set of pots and pans really *will* make "efficiency" our middle name. We'll have everything we need right at our fingertips when we entertain the Mormon Tabernacle Choir for a sit-down dinner!

Then there's the $29.99 mop (a *mop* for heaven's sake!) with 2,999 detachable pieces that will reach into places even your mother-in-law wouldn't think to look. Can't live without that!

And as for that mega-candle deal with all those jelly jars full of fake smells (from cinnamon-asparagus to apple-Right Guard), don't even get me started! I can only wonder where in the world these are made and what they're made of. And might the scent wafting through our homes be a precursor to something far more ominous, like when they add the poisonous gasses?

Here's a tip: The only smell your family really appreciates is real food. Pitch the candles and throw an onion in a pot of hot water 15 minutes before dinnertime. Let the aroma fill the house! It will fool them until it's time to sit down at the table, and by then—being the ingenious person you are—you'll have thought of something to serve for dinner. (Of course, if you want 'em to think you've been cleaning house all day, a dab of Lemon Pledge behind each ear will create the illusion you're hoping for.)

The point is, let's spend our brain power thinking up excuses to get out of work and forget all those timesavers that in actuality take longer and make our lives more complicated.

I found these disclaimers online. They work for me. You're welcome to try them out:

"I don't do windows. I love the birds and don't want one to run into a clean window and get hurt."

"I don't wax floors because I'm terrified a guest will slip and get hurt and sue me."

"I don't mind the dust bunnies because they're very good company. In fact, I've named them and they agree with everything I say."

"I don't spring clean because I love all the seasons and don't want the others to get jealous."

"I don't pull weeds in the garden because I don't want to get in God's way. He's an excellent designer."

Here are two housekeeping tips of my own:

"Be sure to have a large rug in your kitchen, and always wear socks when you cook. Wipe the floor with your socks, and kick the crumbs and gunk under the rug. Deal with it later or not at all."

"To get rid of ants in your kitchen, put sugar on the living room rug."

The bottom line is this: Simplify, dear friend. Simplify!

Even parenting can be simplified. Every word of advice my mother gave me turned out to be true, especially about raising children. When I was expecting my first and trying to wade through stacks of how-to parenting books, she said, "Honey, don't worry so much. Babies come with their own set of instructions."

A book didn't have to tell me how to handle it the first and only time Dana ever lied to me. My God-given instincts told me to wedge a bath-size bar of Dial soap into her dainty little five-year-old mouth and twist, causing soap to cling to her teeth in great gobs.

Did it work? Ask Dana. She'll tell you that to this day, whenever the temptation comes to tell even the slightest, most innocuous fib, she tastes Dial soap and gags. I'm proud to say she's one of the most truthful women you'll ever meet.

Mother also said (Wait! Have I become my mother?) that your instincts come from God and you can trust them. Right now my instincts are telling me to advise you to sell your parenting books for a nickel apiece in a garage sale to some other naïve parent. Or put them in the trunk of your car for the next time it snows—the extra weight will give you better traction.

Okay, okay! Don't look so shocked. Books can be helpful, but for heaven's sake, don't fall for all that child psychology stuff, hook, line and sinker. It's not gospel. And it only gives you guilt if you can't live up to it.

For instance, one of the first things those child-rearing books will tell you is, *Be consistent.* And right off the bat, I must take issue! I say consistency is an overrated, unrealistic virtue. It will make a sane parent crazy and an already-crazy parent crazier!

Who do you know that's consistent? And think about this: Life itself isn't consistent. If you're consistent with your children when they're small, they'll grow up to expect it. What will happen when the PMS years roll around? I say, Keep 'em guessing! Move them into a new bedroom while they're at school. Trade the dog for a cat—or vice versa.

My parents knew how to cut to the chase. They would've been appalled at this Supernanny stuff of tricking the kids into going to bed, making them think they've made the decision themselves: "Would you like a cookie before you go to bed?" In his head, the kid is thinking: *Bed? Where'd that come from? I hadn't planned to go to bed at all! Cookie? Maybe I'll have the cookie now and then throw a fit.*

Yes, my mama and daddy would probably get the electric chair in this day and age for their child-rearing techniques—and believe me "rearing" is the right word for it, if you know what I mean! "No" meant no, and "sit down and hush" meant sit down and hush. "Go to bed" didn't mean let's all have a cookie and a glass of chocolate milk.

As a kid, I had no doubt that my daddy would have taken serious action had I lied, stolen or cheated on a test—or, God forbid, gotten pregnant! We knew what a good spanking was in our family, and my brothers and I turned out quite well, if I do say so myself.

My folks were quite proud of their parenting skills. They were quick to point out how much they loved us. So much so that when they spanked us, it hurt them more than it did us. That's love! (No, wait! Let me think that one over.) I suppose the moral of the story is: If brainwashing works to a parent's advantage, go with it!

Sometimes my own "give it to 'em straight," no-nonsense parenting techniques backfired. Like the time I took Mindy to a fancy lunch with a rather prim and proper friend who said—when a babysitter was not to be had—"Oh, bring her along! She's always so well-behaved."

And until that very day, Mindy had been well-behaved. In fact, she'd been an absolute angel whenever we took her any-where. But on that day, on the drive to the fancy-schmantzy restaurant, my angel-daughter grew horns. She was horrible! She whined, she complained, she interrupted and she got on my last nerve—like fingernails scraping across a blackboard.

When we arrived at our destination, I pulled my precious tyrant aside, gently took her little arm in my hand (okay, in my viselike grip) and through my teeth, I sweetly said (okay, snarled), "If you don't straighten up right now, I'm going to knock your teeth down your throat."

Mindy did the only thing she could think of. She shrieked! It soon became a showdown, and I would be the loser!

When I dared to look up from what I hoped had been a pri-vate mother-daughter moment, there, to my utter shock, were a dozen or more horror-stricken faces peeking over the hedge from the garden-seating section of the restaurant. With an audience now in full view, Mindy seized her moment in the spotlight and gave her best performance. It was Oscar-worthy, if I do say so myself.

"Mama! Oh, Mama! Puh-leeze don't knock my teeth down my throat! I'll be good. I promise, I'll be good!"

At this point I'm sure you're judging me. So I was a bad mother, and for a brief moment I felt guilty for losing my cool.

I've gotten over it.

Parenting has definitely gotten out of hand. What's all this running here and there in your big SUV gas guzzler with a built-in DVD player packed with enough programming to keep the kids happy from Walla Walla, Washington to the other Washington?

Everybody is run ragged. Join this! Join that! Home schooling, private schooling, music lessons, dance lessons, karate instructions, tumbling, rock climbing and kayaking!

My advice? Take them to obedience school and forget the rest! What we're doing is stupid!

But here's something that's dumber than dirt: We're not even supposed to *say* "stupid" anymore! Someone deemed it politically incorrect, and its use has been banned from homes and classrooms across the nation. (I did check the dictionary and it's still there, thank God. And it means "foolish and senseless." As in, "Crossing the street without looking is stupid." As in, "Athletes jamming needles in their behinds is stupid." Don't you think it's a teensy weensy bit *stupid* not to be able to use the word "stupid" when something is, in fact, stupid? Given the chance, I could use it correctly in every other paragraph!)

Here's something else that's politically incorrect: laying a guilt trip on your child. Why do we as mothers so readily accept culpability for the whole family's behavior, but let everyone else off the hook?

I say, Why wallow in guilt, when you can spread it around evenly?

Jewish mothers have been controlling their kids through generous applications of guilt for centuries. To those of us who aren't Jewish, how this technique works is something of a mystery, but we all know it does.

Our family has proof. My daughter dated the suh-weetest, kindest, funniest Jewish boy you'd ever want to know—and yes, we objected because of the differences in our faith. I quietly bit my lip and prayed.

His mother objected for the same reasons we did. But instead of biting her lip, she threw her body prostrate on the floor of her boutique, beat her ample, pearl-laden breast, and *Woe-is-me*'d to the synagogue and back. She heaped on the guilt like lox on bagels. And it worked!

Our children did not marry, and I'd like to be able to testify to the fact that my prayers—the fervent prayers of a righteous woman and all that—changed the course of history. But I have to be truthful. It was more likely *his* mother's time-honored tactics that worked. It was the guilt!

So here's my thinking. Jewish mothers have done it all along, and you can't argue with success. It's time to reverse the guilt flow and get it going back in the direction God intended—toward our kids!

Please hear my heart on this one, dear friend: The time-worn ideal of focusing on the family has often in reality become "focus on the children." I believe that children who've been the "center of the universe" have a misplaced sense of identity and an unreal expectation of entitlement. When they grow up, they'll either have a "the world revolves around me" attitude, or they'll face failure when they find out they aren't as wonderful as they thought they were.

This next remark may be even touchier than the last. Just bringing it up may get me a few nasty letters. So maybe I won't. But then again, shouldn't I just throw it out there and let you decide? No, I'd better not . . . everybody will put me on their prayer list. But hey! That might be a good thing. I need prayer.

Okay, here goes!

My observation is that there are many of us who get carried away going from Bible study to Bible study—spending hours on end filling in the blanks in workbooks. Sometimes it seems like some of us are more intent on learning all the facts about "the whole armor of God" than we are in soaking in the off-the-charts, wonderful truth that it's already ours! We're covered. For heaven's sake, let's *revel in it!*

God gave us such simple instructions: "Serve those who can't repay you," "Go to your closet and pray," "Pray without ceasing," and "Feed the poor." The Ten Commandments, the Lord's Prayer and the Twenty-Third Psalm are pretty simple to understand, too.

And here's a directive that's found three times in a row—right after the part about "I am the vine; you are the branches" (John 15:5), which is where most people get stuck. It says, "Be at home in my love." (Hint for the slow or skeptical: That's what "Remain in me" means.)

Be at home in His love! It took me years to see that one, probably because I was one of those who had gotten stuck.

What I'm saying is this: Let's reevaluate what's important and what's not. You can say no to your kids once in a while. (Or often!) Free yourself to focus on something else for a change and don't feel guilty.

It's okay to take shortcuts, okay if the Mormon Tabernacle Choir has to eat KFC on paper plates just once. Go on, watch that QVC woman with the ohhhh-so-caring voice. Go on, curse the darkness, buy the candles and light up the world. *It's your life!*

And it's a good thing—as Martha Stewart would say, a *very* good thing—to go to Bible study. (I'm not implying that Martha goes to Bible study; I'm just making a point.) But obsessive behavior *isn't* a good thing. It's a good thing to simplify both our way of living and our way of thinking. Stop and do the hokey-pokey once in a while for heaven's sake. Seize the day—not the kids, the stuff or the Bible. Hear! See! Feel! Dance! Sing!

And it's a wonderful thing to be quiet. To just "be at home" in God's love. After all, can you think of a greater tragedy than having His Word and missing His voice?

Unleashing Your Inner BHL!

You know what I'm going to say, don't you, dear reader? *Simplify!* Little by little, get rid of the stuff you don't need. Stop buying things you'll never use, and quit going, going, going!

Learn to sit quietly where you can absorb the beauty of nature. Soak it in, if only for brief moments.

And as my mother always said, "Trust your instincts."

Today might be a good day for you to pick up that just-for-fun book you've been meaning to read, pour yourself a lemonade, prop up your feet and tell your kids to get lost. Practice saying: "Don't bother me!" And start looking for opportunities to reverse that guilt!

A Lame, Lousy Limerick

As a mother, you're down in the pits.
If you could, you'd sure call it quits!
Well, reverse all that guilt,
Tell your kids they'll be kilt.
They'll straighten up and do right, I submit.

A Pithy, Provocative Quote

In response to Martha Stewart's suggestion that you stuff
a miniature marshmallow in the bottom of a sugar cone
to prevent ice cream drips, Maxine says:

Just suck the ice cream out of the bottom of the cone, for Pete's sake!
You are probably lying on the couch with your feet up eating it anyway!
MAXINE (THE CRABBY SUPERSTAR OF HALLMARK CARDS)

CHAPTER 16

Look out the Window, There's a Circus Going On!

Unleashing Yourself to Celebrate Pretty Much Anything and Everything

Anyone can gear up for the big stuff—birthdays, Christmas, Thanksgiving, Ground Hog Day (Wait! I've never celebrated Ground Hog Day. It might be fun!)—but it takes a little effort to celebrate the ordinary . . . the mundane . . . the humdrum . . . the everyday.

That can be a challenge. No! Let's face it. It can be down-right hard.

Yet being able to celebrate the little things in life can make the difference between living a joyful life and simply existing.

Yeah, yeah, I know! There are a lot of roadblocks standing in the way of all that joy. Boo-hoo! Boo-hoo!

So first of all, let's all get ourselves in a good mood. A celebrating kind of mood. A Big-Haired Lady state of mind!

Please don't think I'm judging, even if I am (and I am! It's my spiritual gift). It's just that I've known people who've been in a bad mood for so long that they can't quite remember what a good mood feels like, much less how to celebrate. If you're one of those people (heaven forbid, cross my heart and hope to die!), only you can change your outlook on life.

So, turn that frown upside down . . . smile and the world will smile with you . . . snap out of it . . . stop mully-grubbing . . .

keep crying and I'll give you something to cry about . . . and if you don't straighten up, I'm going to knock you into the middle of next week . . . and why? Just because I *said so*, that's why! (Mother? Again?)

I'll admit there are a lot of roadblocks that keep us from our joy. The biggest is "not enough time." Sure, I'd spread the joy—put on a clown suit and visit nursing homes—if there were more hours in the day. I'd slave all afternoon over a take-out menu and create a magical moment for my family—if I just *had* all afternoon.

If it's not one thing, it's another. Right now it's this book that's taking all my time. It's the deadline hanging over my head! It's Kim, my editor, breathing down my neck (perhaps because she's figured out I have a short attention span and knows it's now or never).

For weeks I've been so consumed with writing that it would be a celebration just to have my refrigerator cleaned out! Whoopee for getting rid of all those containers of know-not-what-it-is (make that know-not-what-it-*used-to-be*) take-out. And the molded cheese that looks a lot like plump, fuzzy, dead mice? Cheers! Cartwheels! Good riddance!

I haven't stopped for anything. Well, I did stop yesterday, when I had a life-or-death type of emergency—which I'm sure you'll understand. I chipped a nail changing the ink cartridge in my printer and had to stop right in the middle of a sentence and fly off to Silky Nails, honking for dear life and running more red lights than I could count.

"Help! Help!" I cried, knowing it's one of only a few English words my Vietnamese nail stylist understands. He understands crisis like nobody else I've ever met.

"Seet down, seet down. I feex!" he said, shoving me into a chair and spinning me toward his station.

Besides not having enough time, lack of money can be a roadblock to celebration. Sometimes there really *is* no money for crêpe paper streamers . . . *or* lemonade! And don't you just hate it when someone spouts that platitude "When life hands you lemons, make lemonade" when you can't even afford lemons?

Money or no money, am I the only classy, well-bred (a-*hem*, cough, cough) woman you know who can celebrate almost anything with a hot dog? It's true. I'd rather have a ketchupy, mustardy, cole-slaw dripping, onion-laden hot dog than a steak. Yummmm! Just thinking about it makes me drool all over the keyboard.

I've always loved hot dogs and never more than when I was expecting Dana. Not far from our house was an open-all-night "dog house" called Arnie's. All they sold was—you guessed it!—hot dogs, with all the toppings known to humankind.

Wayne thought he was funny when he bemoaned to anyone who'd listen that Arnie was a poor, pitiful orphan boy who needed our business. Then he'd pause and wait for it to sink in, ready to deliver his punch line. *"Little orphan Arnie!"* he'd say with glee. (I'm hissing and booing right with you!)

Pregnancy, as you may know, dear reader, brings out cravings for things you'd never dream of otherwise—and usually at times of the night when good, law-abiding Christian people should be sleeping.

"Honey! Honey!" I'd say, "Wake up!" (Grumble, grumble.) "Oh, please! I'm dying—starving to death! Oh, please wake up!"

With that, the inert form next to me would slowly turn over and heave a whooshing sigh proportionate to the bear-like size of his anatomy.

"It's one-thirty. It's cold. It's below zero. Eat some crackers. Eat anything! Just don't make me get out of bed . . . *again!*"

But the words didn't ring true, nor did the pitiful way in which they were delivered. This was a man resigned to the task at hand. He had the routine down pat. He could manage it with one eye shut and one hand holding up his pajama bottoms.

And to his credit, he never mentioned the five flights of steps down to the street and back.

Before I knew it, my watermelon-shaped stomach was balancing a hot dog (sometimes two) with the works. And guess who else's stomach was balancing a hot dog with the works? French fries were shared, and more often than not, a chocolate milkshake. (This was long before gaining weight was a no-no for pregnant women. Ah! The good old days!)

Later we discovered the famous Portillo's dog, and to this day when we fly to Chicago, it's the first place we go, straight from the airport! Between trips I have to make do with my own version of the Chicago dog: Hot-Diggitty-Dog here in Nashville runs a pretty close second.

The point is, life is full of celebration opportunities. Some as simple as eating a hotdog with someone you love.

When I ask my brother Jon and my niece Kirby what comes to mind whenever the word "celebrate" is mentioned, they give each other a knowing look and bust out laughing.

"Cocktail weenies!" they answer in perfect unison.

"No, seriously," I say, "what do you think of?"

"Cocktail weenies!" they repeat, as one voice. One very loud voice!

"Really," I say, "I'm . . ."

"We know. You're writing a book," chuckles my brother. "But really, and I do mean really—"

Kirby takes her cue and again they shout: "Cocktail weenies!"

"Here's what is so great about cocktail weenies," says my wise-beyond-her-years niece. "You buy a big package of cocktail weenies at Sam's Club, the kind with oozing red sauce oozing between its toes . . ." (*toes?*) " . . . and you serve them at your Christmas party."

"Nobody eats 'em," continues my brother, "so you stick 'em in the freezer till the next party . . . and the next . . . and the next.

Each time, you pull 'em out, heat 'em up and serve 'em again."

"When your friends invite you to their parties, you say, 'Oh, I'll bring the cocktail weenies! No, I insist. No trouble at all,'" instructs Kirby. "One package of cocktail weenies can last a whole year."

My brother nods his head in agreement. "No one would think of having a party without cocktail weenies! Again, wrap 'em up and take 'em home. And hi-de-ho, hi-de-ho, back in the freezer they go."

Then, as an afterthought, Kirby adds, "Next Christmas, though, you should throw them out and start over again."

By this time I've forgotten what the original question was.

Oh yeah, I know. "What do you think of when the word 'celebrate' is mentioned?"—and it proves my point! The first thing you think of is food. And the second thing is, you don't have to spend a lot.

Which doesn't change the fact that I like to anyway.

This brings up credit cards. I lost mine—all of them! And my husband didn't even report them missing. No problem, he said. "Whoever found them couldn't possibly charge as much as you do."

Yes, we overuse credit cards. Our excuse is that we like to accumulate mileage so we can travel; and when we travel, we charge more on our cards so we can accumulate more mileage so we can travel . . . Well, you get the picture. It's a vicious cycle. Perhaps you're feeling smug—and rightly so if you've cut up your cards like the experts tell you to do. My question would be, Do you not feel any guilt at all, knowing that the entire economy could fall apart because of your wise thinking?

We've had our share of break-the-bank memories at fancy places, and usually thanks to credit cards. We savor those times and relive them over and over again.

"Remember Chanteclair in Indy? The filet mignon sautéed and flambéed table side with mushrooms and sauce espagnole? The pecan-encrusted trout? The cherries jubilee? The strolling violinist whom Bob paid off if he would just go away? Monell's at Christmas? The strolling madrigals? Kostas in Chicago? Tavern on the Green in New York City and the horse and carriage ride afterward?"

We also connect good times to people. Dear reader, do you get it? Are you seeing the big picture here? *People! Food! Celebration!*

And not always with credit cards.

For example, a big party at Gloria's almost always involves soup and a big basket of unforgettable muffins and breads. At Carlana's, spaghetti is *de rigueur*. It's like none other I've ever tasted, and if she decided to serve some other entree, we'd be downright disappointed. A good time at Alice and Joe's would not be a good time at all if we didn't have Alice's German chocolate cake. Carlene is without question the queen of graham cracker pie, while Bonnie's can't-live-without-it specialty is apple pie. Cousin Diane is at her best when it comes to potato salad. Evelyn is known for her gumbo. And at Kay's, you can count on two things: a big, hungry crowd and *elk* (she lives in Montana and Randy hunts)—cooked every way possible, all at one meal! Elk roast, elk burgers, elk chicken-fried steak—or whatever you call it when it's the same recipe but you replace the chicken with elk—and yes, elk balls. Calm down, it's not what you think! It's ground elk meat, prepared like you'd fix ordinary meatballs.

Getting away from the subject of food (reluctantly, I might add), have you ever thought about celebrating chemotherapy? Whoa . . . that's a whiplash!

My friend Joy—the same Joy who taught me to write and all about gardening (ha, ha, ha . . . NOT!)—taught me how to celebrate chemotherapy. (I always say Joy could celebrate a dead dog.

I just don't want to be the dog.) After every chemo treatment, Joy would show up with a gift. A book. A silly hat. Once it was animal crackers that we shared sitting on the floor in my office.

"Another thing behind us!" she'd say. "Let's celebrate."

And she promised me if I'd live, she would give me an all-expense-paid vacation in the Cayman Islands. Hey, with a promise like that, how can you *not* stay alive? Joy kept her promise, and it was that trip and the spirit of celebration that came with it that revitalized me—and made me ready to face life again.

I know what you're doing, dear reader. You're adding up the cost of a trip like that. That mental calculator of yours is going a mile a minute. The price of the airplane ticket, a condo for a week, food, cabanas on the beach, tips for the cute attentive beach boys, parasailing, snorkeling, an all-day sailing trip, more tips for the cute beach boys—yep, we did it all! You're thinking anybody could celebrate if they had the money—or a friend like Joy. And I agree! It hasn't escaped me that I'm fortunate to have friends who have the means to lavish goodness on others, friends who are off-the-charts generous. It also occurs to me that they *have* much because they *give* much—and because they acknowledge the source of goodness: that every good and perfect gift comes from God.

Sometimes we forget that the best things in life are free, that nature—the very handiwork of the great God of the universe—is free and cause for celebration. The year I was having intense chemotherapy, I began to appreciate what I saw from my own window. On a cold, dreary winter's day, I wrote:

> Today I see a paper sculpture as I look across the landscape—monochromatic grays, not a color in sight. Before I would have said, "Such a gray, gray day." Today I say, "If it were possible to capture this, I could sell it to a king."

Another time I wrote:

"It's a dull, dreary day," they say. Dear God—it's a day!

Yet another time I wrote:

My favorite season is spring. No, it's summer. No, it's
winter! No . . . no, I'm sure it's fall! My friend Gloria
calls the colors of fall "the circus of autumn." I wish I'd
said that! It's the perfect description for this stunning-
ly beautiful and vibrant time of year.

As a traveler, I've often had the good fortune to witness
autumn repeating itself over and over. Long before there's even
a hint of a change in the air in Tennessee, I've peeked from airplane windows—flying over Michigan, Ohio, West Virginia and
Pennsylvania—and caught my breath at the sight of the giant
tapestry of color covering the earth beneath me.

Back on the ground, it's even more magnificent! There, the
raging colors of autumn provide a glorious showcase for the
stuff of everyday life—city folk in richly hued fall wardrobe,
walking through foliage-heavy office parks. Families in bright
sweaters in front yards with rakes in hand—or on porches carv-
ing pumpkins and hanging ghosts and goblins for Halloween.

Pumpkins? What was God thinking when He made pumpkins? Pumpkins still on the ground, snug in the husks of their
basket-like cradles. Or did He picture them on front porches,
with eyes, noses and mouths? Made into pumpkin pies, perhaps?
With rings of brown sugar and pecans, and served with freshly
whipped cream?

Did He plan that unforgettable day for me in Pennsylvania?
Did He know I'd practically wreck my rental car admiring the
work of art He'd created—an overlay of beauty that could only

have been accomplished by a master painter? A pumpkin field tight against the highway. Then, at exactly the right moment, on a dirt road running parallel to the pumpkin field, Amish buggies pulled by sturdy gray workhorses and driven by men in wide-brimmed hats pulled low over their eyes—intentionally, I suppose, to block the sight of the big, green John Deere tractor working the field beside them and, in so doing, shun the conveniences of the modern world.

It was a visual feast for my spirit. The crisp autumn day. The pumpkin field. The Amish buggies with bearded drivers. *Simplicity.* The John Deere behemoth. *Exertion and ambition.* And finally, a backdrop of ruddy woods, highlighted by the touch of God's brush strokes, the exact color of pumpkins but with a few shades of gray and John Deere-green thrown in!

I had no camera, but that Pennsylvania landscape is forever etched in my mind. I call it "A Study in Contrasts." It's as treasured as the Monets and Cassatts that hang in the galleries of my summer villa.

Wait! I saw that look! You're thinking *originals*, right? Adding up price tags again, right? I can hear you muttering, "Wonder how much those cost? Probably more than my whole house. Charged to her credit cards, no doubt."

W-R-O-N-G! To set the record straight, my famous paintings are prints. P-R-I-N-T-S! I don't have even a single gallery! Or a summer villa. Or a winter villa for that matter. If you'll remember from a previous chapter, the only villa I've set foot in is the one where I get my hair done.

Face it, dear reader: *Some of the best things in life are free!* Have you looked around you? Have you savored what you see? Made notes? Gotten out your camera? Told your friends? Thanked God? On your knees?

My friends who have the means to take fancy trips to exotic places, travel on private jet planes, luxuriate in five-star hotels—

some who own cowboy ranches the size of San Francisco!—all learned to celebrate long before they had wealth. And here's why . . .

(Lean in close and pay attention.)

Celebration is an attitude. Not an attitude of *taking*, but of *giving* and of *sharing*. Sort of like, if you share your cocktail weenies when you're poor, you'll share your caviar and *foie gras* when you're rich.

Funny thing is, come to think of it, my rich friends still seem to prefer cocktail weenies.

Wait. Hang on . . . my husband's interrupting.

Okay, I'm back, but I gotta go. I had so much more to say on this subject, but Wayne just came running in, waving an invitation to the grand opening of Costco.

"Call Peggy! Call Alice and Joe, and let's make it a party!"

With a little luck, they'll be handing out samples of cocktail weenies.

Unleashing Your Inner BHL!

Celebrate! Dead dogs! Hot dogs! Cocktail weenies! Caviar! Use credit cards. Don't use credit cards. Crêpe paper, no crêpe paper. With friends, without friends.

Celebrate Ground Hog Day or every day. Use the birthday plate if you must! Go out to a fancy restaurant or make cupcakes at home. Whatever!

Above all, look out the window for Pete's sake! There's a circus goin' on!

A Lame, Lousy Limerick

Look around you and check out the view
Or call friends and invite in a few!
An elk you could carve,

You don't have to starve
Celebrating is not hard to do!

A Pithy, Provocative Quote

The best remedy for those who are afraid, lonely or unhappy is to go outside, somewhere where they can be quiet, alone with the heavens, nature and God. Because only then does one feel that all is as it should be and that God wishes to see people happy, amidst the simple beauty of nature.

ANNE FRANK

CHAPTER 17

I'm Out of Sacred Cows, So Maybe It's Time to Put This Book Out to Pasture

Unleashed to be the Real You, You Big-Haired Lady, You!

No more sacred cows, I promise! How about a wise mouse?

A mouse looked through the crack in the wall to see the farmer and his wife opening a package. "What food might this contain?" He was devastated to discover it was a mousetrap. Retreating to the farmyard, the mouse proclaimed the warning. "There is a mousetrap in the house! There is a mousetrap in the house!"

The chicken clucked and scratched, raised her head and said, "Mr. Mouse, I can tell this is a grave concern to you, but it is of no consequence to me. I cannot be bothered by it."

The mouse turned to the pig and told him, "There is a mousetrap in the house."

The pig sympathized but said, "I am so very sorry, Mr. Mouse, but there is nothing I can do about it but to pray. Be assured that you are in my prayers."

The mouse turned to the cow. She said, "Wow, Mr. Mouse. I'm sorry for you. But it's no skin off my nose."

So the mouse returned to the house, head down and dejected, to face the farmer's mousetrap alone. That very night a sound was heard throughout the house like the sound of a mousetrap catching its prey.

The farmer's wife rushed to see what was caught. In the darkness she did not see that it was a venomous snake whose tail the trap had caught. The snake bit the farmer's wife.

The farmer rushed her to the hospital and she returned home with a fever. Now everyone knows you treat a fever with fresh chicken soup, so the farmer took his hatchet to the farmyard for the soup's main ingredient.

But his wife's sickness continued, so friends and neighbors came to sit with her around the clock. To feed them, the farmer butchered the pig.

The farmer's wife did not get well. She died, and so many people came for her funeral that the farmer had the cow slaughtered to provide enough meat for all of them.

So next time you hear that someone is facing a problem and think that it doesn't concern you, remember that when one of us is threatened, we are all at risk. In the book of Genesis, Cain said about Abel his brother to our God: "Am I my brother's keeper?"

We are all involved in this journey called life. We must keep an eye out for one another and be willing to make that extra effort to encourage one another.[1]

Being the Big-Haired Lady isn't "all about me." It's about being aware and tuned in to others. It's about being a servant to those who cross your path.

I'm often asked, "I never know what to do when someone is sick. Or when there's a crisis in the family, what should I do?"

My response? "Do *something*! Do what you do best." If you're a good cook, take food. Duh! If you don't mind cleaning duty, clean their house! Double duh! If a person in crisis is desperate for money and you have it, be generous. If you're good at praying, write out your prayers and leave them in the mailbox. (And if your friend is going to NYC to have fun and needs someone to go along, go! Do I have to tell you twice?)

Do *something* for goodness sake!

The very next morning after I wrote what you just read, I got a call that Evelyn's condo had burned—as had the entire complex of 20 homes. When I saw the raging fire on the news, I wondered how anyone could have been saved. Evelyn, her son and grandchild were unscathed, but their possessions were ruined by fire and water.

Immediately people from the church pitched in to take charge, and since I had just written the paragraphs above, I thought I should practice what I preach.

Let's see. What do I do best? I asked myself. And then a light bulb came on over my head. (I'm sorry to use myself as the "perfect" example, but it just worked out that way.)

"Shop! That's what I do best!" I cried. However, it then occurred to me that since I've been sitting at this computer writing for days on end, my shopping skills might have gotten pretty rusty. Thus, a secondary benefit became obvious. Shopping would serve two purposes. One for me and one for Evelyn. I'd be able to hone my shopping skills and . . . what was the other thing? Oh yeah . . . Evelyn! (I'm joking! I'm joking!)

My assignment (from Lynn, who was in charge) was to shop for underwear and sleepwear. Soon, I got another phone call saying, "Thank you anyway, but someone else will be buying the underwear." They said I shouldn't give it another thought. "Really, really! Not another thought!"

"Buy the sleepwear but not the underwear. Definitely not the underwear," they said. "Got it?"

It's like they didn't trust me—which, I found out later, they didn't.

I've since learned that in that short, twinkling-of-an-eye time period between the first and second phone calls, a meeting of the church fathers (and maybe some mothers) had been assembled, a vote taken, a resolution written, and a declaration signed and put forth that said:

> Whereas, wherefore, hereto and forevermore, on this the day of our Lord, Suzanne Buchanan shall not now, or ever, under any circumstance, for any reason, be put in charge of, and/or be a participant in the buying of underwear for any and all congregants, missionaries, homeless persons or fire victims including the horses that might have been ridden up upon.

This document was eventually slid under my door at 3 A.M. with a handwritten note that said I'd better watch my backside if I didn't follow the ruling of the church. It was signed with a smiley face, whatever that means. It was probably Evelyn's doing. It would be like her. (She wins the prize, hands-down, for being the number one Big-Haired Lady of all time. Although she's had tragedies galore, she's always looking out for everyone else and finding joy in impossible situations. She spreads the BHL gospel wherever she goes.)

Not long ago I ran across these words to a hymn:

> Brother (sister!) let me be your servant.
> Let me be as Christ to you.
> Pray that I might have the grace
> To let you be my servant, too.

We are pilgrims on a journey.
We are brothers (sisters!) on the road.
We are here to help each other
Walk the mile and bear the load.
I will hold the Christ-light for you
In the night time of your fear.
I will hold my hand out to you;
Speak the peace you long to hear.
I will weep when you are weeping.
When you laugh, I'll laugh with you.
I will share your joy and sorrow
'Till we've seen this journey through.[2]

A true BHL will be all of that. (Evelyn is!) She'll be there in the good and the bad. She'll take up the slack for a sister, and she'll see the journey through. She's in it for the long haul.

A BHL will understand the give and take of it, and know you can't be every single thing to every single person. She's not just a giver, but is gracious when she's on the receiving end.

A BHL accepts the gifts that are offered her and gathers them up one by one and puts them in a big basket (figuratively speaking, of course). She recognizes both the tangible (chocolate, bubble bath, flowers, macaroni casserole) as well as those you can't really touch or see (humor, joy, good conversation, touching, crying, listening), but which are valuable beyond measure. She especially appreciates the gift of time! She even understands that if someone of a different religion or lifestyle offers to pray for you, you should say thank you from the heart and let God sort it out.

A BHL savors her treasure trove of gifts, and she's intentional in keeping the baskets of her friends and acquaintances filled to overflowing.

A BHL is anxious to connect her friends to each other, always widening the circle. "Hey, Carolyn, you should meet Dianna;

you'd love each other. Let's all do lunch." There is great joy in connecting people. Connecting Bonnie and Dana with Kay—and Kay connecting me with Cyndi—made for an unforgettable trip to New York City recently. (I do have to keep checking with Kay as to whether or not, now that I've made these introductions, she still likes me best. She always says the right answer, but sometimes she puts her hand behind her back, which makes me wonder if she has her fingers crossed.)

Jealousy is a big no-no for a BHL. Nope! Not an option! I could write a whole book on the destruction jealousy can cause. If that's your problem, here's a suggestion: Put a rubber band around your wrist, and every time you even *think* in that direction, snap the rubber band. Snap it till it hurts.

It may not cure you of it, but it sure will make you think twice!

When you reach out to others, you'll never be bored. And think about this: might the word "bored" . . . I've saved this until the last chapter . . . here goes . . . argue with me all day, you who have stuck with me until now . . . I think I'm right! Might the word "bored" be interchangeable with the word "selfish"? I'm saying it's so! And once again, it's my book.

Another thing to ponder: Is it possible that when a person continually tells you how tired she is or has an unending list of health complaints (with details that go on *ad nauseam*), might that be her way of saying that she's bored . . . or selfish?

Eeek! Are you mad at me? Agree? Disagree? Well, if the shoe fits . . . you know the rest! (And smack your teenager up the side of the head the next time he tells you he's bored.)

The antidote to boredom is to get involved with something outside your present paradigm. Go do a good deed or six. And vary your route getting there, for Pete's sake. And vary your route getting there, for Pete's sake. And vary your route getting there, for Pete's sake. And vary your route getting there, for Pete's sake. (No, that's not a misprint. I'm just showing you what a rut you can get into if you keep doing the same thing over and over again.)

A BHL would never drive the same route over and over! She'd take in an alligator farm, visit the snake charmer, shop TJ Maxx and manage a few other side trips she'd never even dreamed of until she saw the sign.

A BHL is never, ever bored! Muddleheaded sometimes, but never bored!

Oh, my goodness, where has the time gone? There's so much more to say, but then again, as my friend Peggy says, I've already told you more than I know.

I hope I've given you some things to think about. Some of it I'm beginning to question myself. Like the part about simplifying. What was I thinking? And I told you to be nice to people who were mean to you, to return evil with good. Ha, ha, ha, ha! Is it too late to rethink some of that stuff? I'm even pondering the gold lamé issue. Maybe it *isn't* the new black. Perhaps silver lamé is.

And I hope by now you'll agree with me that all Big-Haired Ladies don't tease their hair up to Jesus. Some of my favorite BHLs have flat hair, thin hair or no hair. I know plenty in the "no hair" category, who've lost their hair because of cancer treatment. Believe me, they're no less BHLs for their lack of hair! Most of them are squeezing everything they can get out of life—and appreciating it more than the rest of us. They're wearing wigs, cute funky ball caps, big earrings and dramatic, Harley-Davidson head wraps, or flowing Joan Crawford scarves. (Joan Crawford had a reputation for being meaner than a junkyard dog, but you'll have to admit, the scarves were quite smashing.)

Big-Haired Lady is an attitude! A cute, darlin', witty, intelligent, passionate, authentic, interesting, "wow—look at me because I'm God's very best creation," seize-the-day *attitude*!

And she's wearing a feather boa, of course.

I hate to say good-bye, so I won't. I'll just say, as one of the ladies at the beauty shop always says, *Boi-nnng voyage!*

Unleashing Your Inner BHL!

Here's a little prayer that I'm saying for all of you dear readers out there! I hope that the God of the universe brings you into the light—the Big-Haired Lady spotlight.

Dear God,

Now that the book is finished, I'm sending prayers heavenward for all my precious new Big-Haired Lady girlfriends.

Let each one wake up every morning to view life with new eyes—with the excitement of a child—and to celebrate the moment.

May she be unleashed from the things that are holding her back: from other people's expectations, from trying to be perfect, from body insecurity, from ruts, guilt, life-sucking friends, naysayers, fear, addictive cycles, boredom, jealously and bad relationships.

God, don't let her get impatient in the process, understanding that a BHL attitude doesn't happen overnight. Sometimes it happens slowly, over time. Perhaps over a lifetime.

Give her peace and comfort regardless of circumstances. And don't let whatever she's going through hold her back, but rather, let it be the very thing that propels her forward to a richer, fuller life in You.

Amen

A Lame, Lousy Limerick

My brain is so taxed; I can only say "Whew!"
At least I admit it and say what is true.
I wish I knew more, but I can't and I don't

And I shouldn't and couldn't and probably won't
If you do and you will . . . then more power to you!

A Pithy, Provocative Quote

Don't take yourself so seriously!
MARY JANE DAVIS (MY MOTHER)

Notes
 1. Rowland Croucher, "The Mousetrap," © John Mark Ministries. http://jmm.aaa.net.
    au/articles/15111.htm, accessed March 2007. Used by permission.
 2. Richard Gillard, "The Servant Song," © 1977 Scripture In Song (c/o Integrity
    Music), c/o Integrity Media, Inc., Mobile, AL. Used by permission.

Epilogue

Being the Big-Haired Lady doesn't happen overnight. It happens slowly, over time. Perhaps over a lifetime. It's simply waking up every morning to view life with new eyes. It's celebrating the moment. It can take place even in the midst of the most discouraging—even devastating—of circumstances.

How do I know? I'll tell you.

I had just signed the contract for this book when my Dana was diagnosed with breast cancer. Again! She had been cancer-free for seven years. This time it reared its ugly head on the opposite side of her body. Apparently, this had nothing to do with the first bout of cancer—and there's a mere 3 percent chance of that happening. And my Dana had taken every precaution, including having both breasts removed and following a sensible plan of nutrition and exercise. Go figure!

I was sure my head would explode, sure my heart was fractured in a million pieces, and I went back and forth from feeling as though my mind was full of crazed killer bees to being helplessly numb from head to toe.

I knew I couldn't possibly write this book. I would cancel. It would be impossible to deliver a manuscript of any sort under the circumstances, much less a humorous one.

A day or two after the diagnosis, my husband and I got in the car and drove to Ohio to spend the weekend with Dana and Barry. Our spirits were heavy. We felt a sense of helplessness, of hopelessness. How could we possibly encourage them when our own resources were so depleted? We tried to steel ourselves, to prepare for what we thought would be the worst weekend of our lives.

It was not to be.

It's hard to explain, but it turned out to be one of the best, most spirit-enriching—fun?—times we'd ever known together.

Later, we found ourselves referring to those few days as "golden moments," recalling a togetherness that possibly would never have happened had it not been for the diagnosis.

Did we cry? Did we sob? We did. And we hugged a lot. And sat on the porch under blankets and talked long hours, said things we'd never said before.

We laughed a lot! The kind of laughing I spoke about earlier in the book, where you just let go and let it overwhelm you (and make you run for the bathroom!). We watched a funny movie and it tickled us right down to our toes.

We listened to music together, and Dana and I knitted cozily and visited a new yarn shop and planned future projects. She went off to play her harp for a wedding, while Wayne and Barry (who always says "we" when he refers to what Dana is going through) did odd jobs.

I ran errands. I ran errands because when men do odd jobs, they need to send someone back and forth (with at least $200 in her pocket) to Lowe's and Home Depot.

We ordered in Greek food and savored every bite—and Maria, the darling lady who owns the restaurant (and knew of our recent dilemma) threw in a half-dozen extras, including delicious homemade desserts. She fed our bodies, but even more so, our souls. Wordlessly, Maria's kindness spoke volumes: "I will hold the Christ-light for you, in the night time of your fear."

We prayed. Our prayers were short, and to the casual observer they might have sounded overly abrupt and shallow: "Father in heaven, you know exactly what we're feeling. You're in charge. You helped us do this before, and You can help us again. Let us know the presence of Your Holy Spirit. Your will be done. Amen."

When the subject of this book came up and whether I could possibly deliver it as promised, Dana was the first to speak. "Well, we either believe all that stuff or we don't." (*We*? Who is this *we*

she's talking about? Did I miss something?) "Circumstances
have nothing to do with it, right? You still gotta live life to the
fullest, as though each day were your last. Right? Isn't that what
you taught me?" (Truth is, I never realized she had been listening.) "You still gotta deal with quirky, mean-spirited people,
right? And that 'think I can, think I can' thing—you still believe
that, don't ya? And, Mama, you still gotta laugh! Right?"

Barry was nodding his head in agreement, which would
be natural for Barry since he's the original positive-thinker-
Big-Haired-Lady-Man (not to be confused with a girly-man,
by the way).

I almost fell off my chair at what Dana was saying. That
bratty little kid had never given me a clue she had been pay-
ing attention to anything I ever said! Now here she was parroting me word for word—and doing the very thing she
accused me of doing: jabbing her pointer finger practically
up the nose of whoever was near. (Well, not really, but you get
the picture.)

And here I was, not even sure I believed any of it anymore.

Before the diagnosis, Dana and I had promised to speak for
a breast cancer awareness event at Gaither Family Resources, an
eye-popping, not-to-be-missed-if-you're-within-a-day's-drive
retail store in central Indiana, where you can spend the whole
day shopping, having a gourmet lunch and sitting in big rock-
ers watching the Gaither videos. People drive there from all over
the country, having seen the Gaithers and their Homecoming
troubadours on TV. Fabulous events are held there all the time,
and it's not unusual to find a book signing, a concert or an art
fair going on. (I think I've told you before but I'll tell you again—
you have to check out www.gaitherfamilyresources.com.)

This would be our first speaking engagement together.
It was a joyous, celebratory occasion and it was called PINK,
which everything was, from the stage lighting, to the table

decorations, to most of the attendees, many of whom were cancer survivors.

It's interesting to note that six years before, I had told Dana I thought she had a lot to say and would be a good speaker, to which she firmly replied, "Mother, don't go there! I'm not you. I am *not* a speaker!"

Well, mothers sometimes have to bite their tongues (in this case for six years), but they always turn out to be right. Dana *is* a speaker! A funny, witty speaker. And she's a compelling writer!

Here's what she wrote, and read that night. The women (and a few men) loved her.

Dirty Red Bandanas and the Color Pink

I always hated the color pink.

Maybe it's because pink was precisely the *wrong* color for an aspiring hippie chick like me. Or maybe because—as any girl who came of age in the 1970s could tell you—pink was *nowhere* for a redhead until Molly Ringwald made it oh-so-fashionable.

Back in the '70s, rebellion was all the rage—and clothes were the red flag of rebellion. Being the compliant firstborn child that I was, I wasn't much into rebellion. What was there to rebel against, anyway? Summers at the swim club? Trips to places my friends only read about in books? Parents who thought I was funny and bright, who respected my ideas and treated me like an adult?

Still, mine were the dreams of a revolutionary, and in a family like mine—with a fashion-plate *mother* like mine—clothes were the only surefire way I knew to launch a revolution. Complete with fireworks!

I thought my outfit made quite the statement: Faded Mickey Mouse T-shirt. Fringed bell-bottom jeans. A pair of beat-up Converse sneakers. And over my long, unwashed Karen Carpenter hair, a dirty red bandana. Worn every day. Rain or shine. For an entire summer.

The only time I ditched that outfit was for church. And don't think for a minute it was out of reverence for God! Who needs the fear of God when she has the Fear of Mother?

Speaking of Mother, mine can only be described as a certifiable pink-pusher. "Pink looks wonderful on every-one!" she'd exclaim to my revolutionary junior high self. "*They're all* wearing pink this season." ("Who are *they*?" I'd mumble behind her back. To this day I haven't a clue.)

"Pink gives your complexion *color*," she'd say, her rouge-covered thumb darting like a laser beam right into my personal space, "color you wouldn't need if you'd let me put a *hint* of blush *right here* . . ."

Mama wasn't happy till I looked like cotton candy and felt like a circus peanut.

Most of the breast cancer survivors I know can divide their lives into two distinct periods: BC (before cancer) and AD (after diagnosis). My life can be neatly divided into Pre- and Post-Pink.

Pink is my color now. Pink jammies, pink clogs, and the fab hot-pink poncho I finished knitting just the other day. Sure, my '70s self would roll over in its grave if I donned a pink suit—the kind you'd see on a politician's wife. And Gwyneth Paltrow's pretty-in-pink Oscar gown? (Forget it, Mother. Not on your life!)

But, oh, how I do love pink . . .

Pink is the sandpaper tongue of the cat who kisses me awake every morning.

Pink is the funky ski hat I wore when I plunged down the mountain on my first black diamond run.

Pink is the salmon I caught that summer on Lake Michigan.

Pink is the nubby yarn I knitted into a great scarf for my niece.

Pink is my own cute toenails—peeking up out of sugar-white sand at low tide.

Pink is the streamer that floats to the floor as I kiss my sweet husband on the dance floor. *(Another New Year's Eve and I'm still here!)*

Pink is the girly drink I sipped with my Internet girlfriends that crazy weekend we met "in real life" in Chicago.

Pink is the sunset's reflection on an endless expanse of snow-kissed mountain peaks against a big Montana sky.

Pink is a miracle.

Pink is wonder.

Pink is a call to live my life more fully and courageously than ever before.

Need I tell you that none of this "pinkness" . . . this life-experienced-in-all-its-radiant-fullness . . . even existed for me before cancer?

I'll come right out and say what you may be thinking. Somehow—despite everything inside and outside of us that tries to convince us otherwise—life is better, richer, deeper on this side of a breast cancer diagnosis.

Better because we know what we might be missing. Richer because cancer has taught us to discover what we're made of and all that we have. Deeper for all the stolen moments we've lived. *Lived!*

So which would you choose: a dirty red bandana or the color pink?

I'll take the color pink![1]

Me, too!

A Pithy, Provocative Quote

Life is just so beautiful! When you notice it. And "noticing it" is the strange gift of cancer treatment. It's a gift I never wanted to receive again, but now that I've got it, I'm savoring the moments as they come. And, of course, I'm counting down the moments for "it" to be over! Ha-ha!

DANA BUCHANAN SHAFER
(JUST YESTERDAY IN AN EMAIL)

Note

1. Dana Buchanan Shafer, © 2006 by Dana Shafer. All rights reserved. Used by permission.